Teach Yourself Italian

Teach Yourself
ITALIAN

SAURABH KUMAR

MAHAVEER
PUBLISHERS

Published by
MAHAVEER PUBLISHERS
4764/2A, 23-Ansari Road, Daryaganj
New Delhi - 110002
Ph. : 011 – 66629669–79–89
Fax : 011 – 41563419
e-mail : mahaveerpublishers@gmail.com

© Mahaveer Publishers

First Edition : 2006
Second Revised Edition : 2008
Reprint : 2010

Teach Yourself Italian
ISBN : 9788190219693

Distributed by
VAIBHAV BOOK SERVICE
e-mail : vaibhavbookservice@gmail.com

Published by D.K. Jha for Mahaveer Publishers
Printed by Jaico Printers, New Delhi

Preface

The modern period represents an era of global village due to enormous progress made in the field of electronics and communication. The world has virtually turned into a single commune however to communicate the people of alien country it has became essential to acquire knowledge of one or more of foreign languages by a single person.

The Italian is one of the foreign languages which has got weightage in the international communication as it is well known that Italy is a major country in Europe, in the world as well as for manufacturing automobiles and of immense tourist interest country. It is therefore almost much more desirable to have the basic knowledge of Italian language.

The present efforts through this minimum presentation of Italian language vis-à-vis with other foreign language has been made to acquire a working knowledge of Italian language. It is hoped that the same will be suitable to a learner of Italian language.

Author

Contents

The Alphabets and pronunciation

The Italian Vowels
Aa (आ) is pronounced as 'a' in lather

Amico	Casa	Abito
आमिको	काजा	अबीतो

Ee (ए) This vowel may have a closed sound like in (ऐ) or an open sound like in ऍ choice is present only when e is the accented vowel when it is not accented the sound is always the closed 'e' sound.

Cena	Mese	Mezza
चेना	मेजे	मेज्जा

i (इ) It is pronounced either as इ (Abito) or ई (Piccolo), (according to) whether the stress is on the vowel or not.

India	Impiro	Pilota
इन्दिया	इमपेरो	पिलौता

Oo (ओ) This vowel may have a closed sound like an ओ or an open sound like in औ same like in 'e'.

Oggi	Opposto	Torta	Legno
ओजी	अपोस्तो	तोरता	लेनो

Uu(ऊ) Always has a long ऊ sound

Unita	Unico	Stupido
उनीता	ऊनिको	स्तुपिदो

The Italian Consonants

Bb(बी) Pronounced as 'bi' in 'biscuit'

Banco	Birra	Benzina
बान्को	बिर्रा	बेन्जीना

Cc(चि) The pronunciation of c depends on the letter following it according to that the sound is either क or च.

i) We have the sound क when c is followed by a, o, u, h

ii) We have the sound च when it is followed by e, i.

iii) The combinations "chi" and "che" give the sound की and के

C = क when followed by a, o u, h

Case	Cosa	Cura	China
काजा	कोजा	कुरा	किना

C = च when followed by e, i

Cibo	Cina	Cena	Cera
चिबो	चिना	चेना	चैरा

The combinations of chi and che chi = की

Chirurgia	Chiesa	Chiave
कीरूरगा	किएजा	कियावे
Chi = के	Greche	Stanche
	ग्रेके	स्तान्के

Dd(दी) d is always pronounced as द and not ड like 'd' in Dinner

Diploma	Dio	Fede	Idolo
दिप्लोमा	दियो	फेदे	इदोलो

Ff(एफ) Like 'f' in 'friend' same as in English

Fame	Fista	Difficile	Forte
फामे	फेस्ता	दिफिचिले	फोरते

Gg () The pronunciation of 'g' depends on the letter following it. According to that the sound is either ग or ज

i) We have the sound ग when 'g' is followed by a, o, u, h
example

Gamba	Gomma	Guerra
गाम्बा	गोम्मा	ग्वेर्रा

ii) We have the sound ज when 'g' is followed by e, i
example

Gelato	Gennaio	Giro	Gita
जेलातो	जेनायो	जीरो	जिता

11

iii) The combinations ghi and ghe give two sounds गी and गे

Ghi

Ghiaccio	Chirurghi	Alberghi
धियाचो	किरॉगी	अलबेग्री

Ghe

Larghi	Lunghi
लारगे	लुन्गी

iv) gli, gn = These two sounds have no exact corresponding sound in either English or Hindi
The closest to 'gli' is 'lly' as in billion. The closest to 'gn' is 'nny' and in canyon

gli - consiglio	gn - cognome
कोंसिलियो	कन्नोमे

Hn ( ) = This letter is often used in writing but never pronounced in writing. It is used to distinguish words that have the same sounds but different meanings and creating combinations of letters that correspond to the sounds
chi, che, ghi, glu

Le (एल) used as 'L' in English

Lezione	Dolce	Falso
लेतसिमोने	दोल्चे	फाल्सो

Mm(एमे) used as 'm' in English

Madre	Mano	Ombra
मादरे	मानो	ओम्बरा

Nn(एने) English 'n'

Naso	Natale	Pranzo	Invece
नाजो	नाताले	प्रान्जो	इनवेचे

Pp(प) Like English 'p'

Penna	Pietra	Sport
पेन्ना	पियात्रा	स्पोर्त

Qq(क्यु) Like English 'Q'

Quattro	Quindi	Aqua
कवार्तो	कवीन्दी	आक्वा

Rr(एरे) Pronounced as 'R' in English

Riso	Romanzo	Rima
रिजो	रामांजो	रिमा

Ss(एसे) In some cases 'S' is pronounced as 's' in single
or
in other ज
S + क (ca, co) = स्क
S + च (Ci) = श
like
S + क =	Sconto	Scopa
	स्कोन्तो	स्कोपा

S + च =   Sciopero   Scimmia
           सोपेरो   सिम्मिया

Tt(त) T is always pronounced त and not ट
pronounced 'T' as in 'Arti'
Tempo   Testa   Matallo
तेम्पो   तेस्ता   माताली

Vv( ) = Pronounced 'V' in 'Violence' van in English
Valle   Vaso   Favole   Svezia
वाले   वाजो   फावोले   स्वेत्सीया

Z(त्स दज) = Pronounced 'ts' as in the English 'bets'
and 'dz' as in English 'bids'
(∵ z always has a double consonant sound either त्स
दज)
ts =   Gratzie   Ragazza
             ग्रात्सीया   रगात्सा
dz =   Zanzara   Zero
             जंन्जारा   जेरो
J = i lunga
K = Cappa
W = doppia vu
X = ics
y = ipsilon
These are the letters which do not exist in Italian
Alphabets. They are of no use.

Pronunciation Patterns

In Italian each and every word is pronounced according to its pronunciation. No word carries silent pronunciation as in English.

(a) If a word ends in a vowel, the vowel is stressed

Tempo	= Tāmpo	= तेम्पो
Techologia	= Tēknolozia	= तेक्जोलौजिया
Miraggio	= Mirazzo	= मिराजो
Milza	= Miltsa	= मिल्जा

(b) When the last letter of the word is not accented and it is vowel

(i) The sound is always closed

Ragazzo	Matto	Sedie
रागत्सो	मात्तो	सैदिये

(ii) But when the vowel is accented, it is more open like

città	Perchè	Unità	Università
चित्ता	पेरके	उनिता	उनिवरसिता

Punctuation:

Punctuation in Italian is same to the punctuation of English language.

like

Dove abiti? (Where do you live?) Do-vay a-bi-ti

che sorpreso! (what a surprise!) Kay soor - prēso

Capitalization :

In Italian, capitalization is same as in English.

(i) All nouns are written in big letters

Formation of a Italian Sentence

There are few instructions by obeying them one can learn the language effectively and easily, step by step

(i) Reading out the word to word exactly what is written

(ii) Repeating the words again and again in order to achieve proficiency over the pronunciation of words

(iii) Practicing by reading the words loudly of every reading

Differences between the pronunciation of Italian and the pronunciation of English.

(a) Italian Language is more sweat and Simple language and all the alphabets are pronounced collectively and stressfully.

(b) The intonation of the Italian speech is different from the intonation of English speech. Every language has its own characteristics intonations so does Italian.

(c) The modority of Italian syllables end in a vowel sound and this fact helps you make the difference between the Italian pronunciations & the English pronunciation of the following words.

Italian	pro-fe-ssore	ne-ce-ssa-rio
English	pro-fess-or	nec-e-ssar-y
English Phonetic	profesō-orē	nesesaariio
Italian phonetic	प्रोफेसोरे	नेचेसारियो

(d) Vowels are short and play very important role in Italian language. Most of the words end with the vowels. In Italian the emphasis is purely on the Italian vowels and if the vowels are without accent the pronunciation is open.

(e) Consonants are pronounced with less stress in Italian
- Personal subject pronoun is not necessary to be written. The ending of the verbs itself indicates to whom it refers to.
- The Subject always agrees with number and gender
- For making a sentence negative we just put No/Non before verb in any case.

> Non parlo Italiano
> (I don't speak Italian)

- For making a sentence interrogative we just put the interrogation signs on both the sides. This is one of the important part of Italian]

Parli Italiano?
Do you speak Italian?
Non Parli Italiano?
You Don't speak Italian?

- While making the sentence in the verb we just remove the last three letter of any particular verbs (are, ire, ere) and we add the conjugations of the respective verb.

Parl<u>are</u>	= Parlo	= I speak
Mang<u>iare</u>	= Mangio	= I eat
Viv<u>ire</u>	= Vivete	= You will live
Spend<u>ere</u>	= Spendiamo	= We spend

- To put the stress on any letter or to emphasize it we put out sign (' ') on the letter which is called accent.

Example:

Città	Università	Unità
चित्ता	उनीवरसिता	उनिता

- Passive is less in use

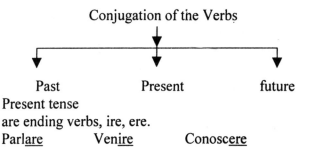

Conjugation of the Verbs

Past   Present   future

Present tense
are ending verbs, ire, ere.

Parl<u>are</u>   Ven<u>ire</u>   Conosc<u>ere</u>

(To speak)	(To come)	(To know)
Andare	Pulire	Sapere
(To go)	(To clean)	(To Know)
Fumare	finire	Spendere
(To smoke)	(To finish)	(To spend)
Mangiare		
(To eat)		
Cominciare		
(To Start)		

Conjugations

	are	ire	ere
Io (I)	o	o	o
Tu (You)	i	i	i
lui/lui (he/she)	a	e	e
Noi (We)	iamo	iamo	iamo
voi (you all)	ate	ite	ete
Loro (They)	ano	ono	ano

Past Tense
In Italian there are three types of past tense which are
used according to the nature of the sentence
(i) Passato prossimo
(ii) Imperfetto
(iii) Passato Remoto

(i) Passato prossimo
       are ending → ito
       Andare → Andato

Mangiare → Mangiato

ire ending → ito
Finire → finito
Spedire → spedito

ere ending → uto
Conosare → Conosciuto
Sapere → Saputo

Auxiliary for Passato prossimo

Avere(to have)	Essere (to be)
Io-ho	Io-sono
Tu-hai	tu-sei
Lui/Lei-ha	lui/lei-è
Noi-abbiamo	Noi-siamo
Voi-avete	voi-siete
Loro-hanno	loro-sono

Essere = Use in verb of motion like Andare, Venire, Uscire, Salire, Scendere tornare, ritornare, cadere etc.
Example
Sono Andato (I went)
Siamo Venutù (We went)

Imperfetto

Io	Andavo	Partivo	Sapevo
Tu	Andavi	Partivi	Sapevi
lui/lei	Andava	Partiva	Sapeva

Noi	andavamo	Partivamo	Sapevamo
Voi	Andavate	Partivate	Sapevate
Loro	Andavano	Partivano	Sapevano

Andavo	(I was going)
	(I used to go)
Partivo	(I was leaving)
	(I used to leave)
Sapeva	(I was knowing)
	(I used to know)

Future Tense

Io/i	=	rò
Tu/You	=	rai
Lui/lei/He/She	=	rà
Noi/We	=	remo
Voi/You all	=	rete
Loro /They	=	ranno

Like

Andare	Partire
Andrò (I will go)	Partirò (I will leave)
Sapere	
Saperò (I will know)	

Subject = First person, Singular number

1. I go.
   vado
   vaado
   वादो

2. I am going.
   sto andando
   Esto - an- daan - do
   स्तो आन्दान्दो

3. I have gone.
   Somo Andato
   sono an-daa-to
   सोनो अन्दातो

4. I have been going since 10 o clock
   vado da 10 A.M.
   vaa-do da
   वादो दा 10 A.M

5. I went.
   Sono andato
   Sono andato
   सोनो आन्दातो

6. I was going.
   Stavo andando.
   Staa - vo - andaan-do
   स्तावो आन्दोन्दो

7. I had gone.
   ero andato.
   ēro-an-daa-too.
   ऐरो आन्दतो

8. I had been going since 2001.
   ero andato da 2001
   ero andato da 2001 ēro-andaa-to.
   ऐरो आन्दातो दा 2001.

9. I will go.
   Andrò
   An-droo
   आन्द्रौ

10. I will be going.
    Sarò andato.
    Sa-roo an-daa-to
    सरौ आन्दातो

11. I will have gone
    Sarei andato.
    saa-rēi-andaa-to.
    सरेई आन्दातो

24

12. I can go.
    poosso andare.
    po-ss-oo an-da-rē.
    पोसो आन्दारे

13. I could go.
    potrei andare.
    pot-rei an-da-rē.
    पोतरेई आन्दारे

14. I will be able to go.
    Sarò andato.
    sa-roo an-daa-to
    सरौ आन्दातो

15. Can I go?
    Posso andare?
    po-ss-oo an-da-rē?
    पोतरेई आन्दारे

16. Could I go?
    Potrei andare ?
    pot-rēi an-da-rè?
    पोतरेई आन्दारे

17. Will I be able to go?
    poterò andare?

potē-roo an-da-rē?
पोतेरौ आन्दारे

18. I want to go.
Voglio andare.
Vo-olio an-da-rē.
वोल्यो आन्दारे

19. **I wanted** to go.
Ho voluto andare.
oō vō-loo-tō a-nda-rē.
ओ बोलुतो आन्दारे

20. I would like to go.
vorrei andare.
vo-rr-ēi an-da-rē.
वोरई आन्दारे

21. I should go/ I must go/ I ought to go.
devo andare.
day-vo an-da-rē.
देवो आन्दारे

Grammar
Tense

Past	**Present**	**Future**
(Pasato)	(Presente)	(Futuro)
I went	I go	I will go
Sono andato	Vado	Andrò
You went	You go	You will go
Sei andato	Vai-yo go	Andrai
We went	We go	We will go
Siamo andati	Andiamo	Andremo
You all went	You all go	You all will go
Siete andati	Andate	Andrete
They went	They go	They will go
sono andati	vadano	andranno
He/She went	He/She goes	He/She will go
è andato/a	Va	Andrà

A Review of Italian Verbs

In Italian language there are two types of verbs

Regular	Irregular
Parlare (To speak) पारलारे	Potere (To be able to) पोतेरे
Cantare (To Sing) कानतारे	Fare (To do) फारे
Scrivere (To Write) स्क्रीवेरे	Venire (To Coan) वेनिरे

Irregular Verbs for past and future

28

Presente	Pasato prossimo Preceded by auxilary	Futuro		
			$+$ Conjugation of future	
Avere	Avuto	Av		
Vedere	Vissuto	Ved		
Dovere	Dovuto	Dov		
Patere	Potuto	Pot		
Volere	Voluto	Vol		
Sapere	Saputo	Sap		
Andare	Andato	And		
Vehire	Venuto	Ver		
Bire	Bevuto irregular	Per		
Dare	Dato irrgular	Da		
Stare	Stato	Sta		
Dire	Detto irregular	Di		

In Italian language the verbs are identified by their ending All the Italian verbs always end up in three or four ways.

- are   parlare   (To Speak)
- Ire   partiere   (To leave)
- ere   Sapere   (To Know)
- esce   finire   (To end)
         finisco
         finisci
         finisce

Subject - Pronoun

Singular	Plural
I (Io)	We (Noi)
You (Tu)	You all (Voi)
He/She (lui/lei/lei)	They (loro)

My   → Mio/a   → our (Nostro) i, a, e
Your   → Tuo/a   → Your (Vostro) i, a, e
Her/his → Suo/a   → Their (Loro) Suoi/e, a, o

* According to subject, number & gender

like

my pen = mia penna
my pens = mie penne

your car = tua macchina
your cars = tue macchine

his book = suo libro
his books = suoi libri

our house = Nostra casa
our houses = nostre casa

your brother = vostro fratello
your brothers = vostri fratelli

(i) In Italian 'Lei' is used for formal on place of 'Tu'

(ii) and 'Lovo' is used for formal on place of 'vai'

Note: In Italian it's always not important to mention out the subject pronoun. Because the conjugation itself of every pronoun is different and clearly indicates whom it refers to

Note: One can use subject pronoun for giving emphasis or stress sometime. for example:

(IO) Parlo Italiano = I Speak Italian
(Tu) Vai a leizione = You go to the lesson

But:
io sono franco = I am Franco

Sono Andato   सोनो आन्दातो
Sei Andato   सेई आन्दातो
E Andato   एइ आन्दातो
Siete Andati   सियेते आन्दाती
Siames Andati   सियामेस आन्दाती
Sono Andati   सोनो आन्दाती

Vado   वादो
Vai   वाई
Va   वा

andiamo अन्द्यामो
andati अन्दाति
vadano वादानो

Andrò आन्द्रो
Andrai आन्द्राइ
Andraà आन्द्रा
andrimo आन्द्रेमो
Andreite आन्द्रेते
Andranno आन्द्रानो

1.	To absorb	= assorbire	= *assorbirē*	= अजोर्बिरे
2.	To accept	= accettare	= *accēttarē*	= अचेतारे
3.	To accompany	= accompagnare	= *akompagnarē*	= अकोम्पंयारे

4.	To act	Ricitare	*ricitarē*	रिचितारे
5.	To add	aggiungere	*ajunjērē*	अजुन्जेरे
6.	To admire	ammirare	*ammirarē*	आम्मिरारे
7.	To advise	raccomandare	*rakomandarē*	रेकोमन्दारे
8.	To agree	essere daccordo	*essērē dākordo*	एस्सेरे दाकोर्दो
9.	To allow	permettere	*pērmēttērē*	पेरमेत्तेरे
10.	To annoy	infastidirsi	*infastidirsi*	इन्फास्तिदिर्सी
11.	To apologize	Chiedere scusa	*kiēdērē skusa*	कीएदेरे स्कुजा
12.	To apply	Applicarsi/kare	*applikarē*	आप्लीकारे
13.	To approach	Avvicinarsi	*avvicinarsi*	अव्विचिनार्सी
14.	To arise	Presentare	*Prēsēntarsi*	प्रेजेन्तार्सी
15.	To arrange	organizzare	*organissarē*	ओरगनित्तसारे
16.	To arrive	Arrivare	*arrivarē*	अरीवारे

35

17.	To ask	=	chiedere	=	*kiēdērē*	=	कीएदेरे
18.	To assist	=	Assistere	=	*assistēarē*	=	अस्सीसतेरे
19.	To assure	=	Assicurare	=	*assikurarē*	=	अस्सीकुरारे
20.	To attach	=	Fissare	=	*Fissarē*	=	फिस्सारे
21.	To attack	=	Attacare	=	*āttacarē*	=	आत्ताकारे
22.	To attempt	=	Tentare	=	*Tēntarē*	=	तेन्तारे
23.	To attend	=	assistere	=	*assistērē*	=	अस्सीसतेरे
24.	To attract	=	Attrarsi	=	*attirarē*	=	अतीरारे
25.	To authorize	=	Autorizzare	=	*auto-ritsarē*	=	ओतो रित्सारे
26.	To awake	=	Svegliarsi	=	*svēl-iarsi*	=	सवेल्यारसी
27.	To able	=	Essere capace	=	*Ēssērē Kapacē*	=	एस्सेरे कापाचे
28.	To ban	=	interdire	=	*intērdirē*	=	इन्तरदिरे
29.	To bargain	=	Affare	=	*affarē*	=	अफारे

36

	English		Italian		Transliteration		Hindi
30.	To bath	=	Fare il bagno	=	*Farē il bano*	=	फारे इल बानो
31.	To batter	=	Battere	=	*battērē*	=	बातेरे
32.	To beat	=	Battere	=	*battērē*	=	बातेरे
33.	To befriend	=	Essere amiko	=	*Ēssēre amiko*	=	एस्सेरे अमीको
34.	To beg	=	Elemosinare	=	*ēlēmosinarē*	=	इलेमोसीनारे
35.	To begin	=	cominciare	=	*kominciarē*	=	कोमीनचारे
36.	To behave	=	comportarsi	=	*Komportarsi*	=	कोम्पोरतारसी
37.	To believe	=	Credere	=	*krēdērē*	=	क्रेदेरे
38.	To bend	=	Piegarsi	=	*piēgarsi*	=	पीएगारसी
39.	To betray	=	denunciare	=	*dēnunaarē*	=	देनुनचारे
40.	To bid	=	fare un'offerta	=	*Farē un offērta*	=	फारे उन ओफेरता
41.	To bite	=	Mordere	=	*mordērē*	=	मोरदेरे

42.	To blast	=	Far saltare	=	*Far saltarē*	=	फार साल्तारे
43.	To bless	=	Benedire	=	*bēnēdirē*	=	बेनेदिरे
44.	To block	=	Blokare	=	*blokarē*	=	ब्लोकारे
45.	To blossom	=	Essere in fiore	=	*Essēre in fio-rē*	=	एस्सेरे इन फ्योरे
46.	To blow	=	Saltare	=	*saltarē*	=	साल्तारे
47.	To bolt	=	bullonare	=	*bullonarē*	=	बुल्लोनारे
48.	To bore	=	Annoiare	=	*annoiarē*	=	अन्नुवारे
49.	To bounce	=	rimbalzare	=	*rimbalsarē*	=	रिम्बलतसारे
50.	To break	=	rompersi	=	*rompērē*	=	रोम्परे
51.	To breath	=	Respirare	=	*rēspirarē*	=	रेस्पीरारे
52.	To brush	=	spazzolare	=	*spatsolarē*	=	स्पातसोलारे
53.	To buy	=	comprare	=	*comprarē*	=	कोम्परारे
54.	To calculate	=	calcolare	=	*kalcolarē*	=	कालकोलारे

38

No.	English		Italian		Transliteration		Hindi
55.	To call	=	Chiamare	=	*kiamarē*	=	क्यामारे
56.	To cancel	=	annullare	=	*Annullārē*	=	अनुलारे
57.	To care	=	Curare	=	*kurarē*	=	कुरारे
58.	To carry	=	trasportare	=	*portarē*	=	पुरतारे
59.	To cash	=	incassare	=	*inkassarē*	=	इनकासारे
60.	To catch	=	cogliere	=	*koliēre*	=	कोलीएरे
61.	To certify	=	certificare	=	*Cērtitifkarē*	=	चेरतीफिकारे
62.	To change	=	cambiare	=	*kambiarē*	=	काम्बीयारे
63.	To chase	=	inseguire	=	*insēguirē*	=	इनसेगवीरे
64.	To cheat	=	Imbroliare	=	*imbroliarē*	=	इम्बुलीयारे
65.	To check	=	controllare	=	*corrēgēre*	=	कोरेजेरे
66.	To choke	=	soffocarsi	=	*soffokarsi*	=	स्फोकारसी
67.	To chop	=	tagliare	=	*taliarē*	=	तालीयारे

39

68.	To choose	=	scegliere	=	*scegliērē*	=	सलीयेरे
69.	To chuckle	=	riso soffocato, ridere sommessamente	=	*ridērē* *sommēssamēntē*	=	रीदेरे सोमेश्शाम्मेन्त
70.	To circulate	=	circolare	=	*cirkolarē*	=	चीरकोलारे
71.	To claim	=	sostenere	=	*sostēnērē*	=	सोस्तेनेरे
72.	To clap	=	applaudire	=	*applaudire*	=	आपलॉदिरे
73.	To clean	=	Pulire	=	*pulirē*	=	पुलीरे
74.	To clerch	=	Stringere	=	*strinjērē*	=	स्त्रीनजेरे
75.	To close	=	chiudersi	=	*kiudērē*	=	क्युदेरे
76.	To collect	=	raccogliere	=	*rakoliērē*	=	रकोलीयेरे
77.	To combine	=	unire	=	*unirē*	=	उनीरे
78.	To come	=	Venire	=	*Vēnirē*	=	वेनीरे

40

79.	To compel	=	costringere	=	kostrinjērē	=	कोसत्रिनजेरे
80.	To complain	=	Lamentare	=	lamēntarē	=	लामेन्तारे
81.	To confide	=	Confidare	=	konfidarē	=	कोनफीदारे
82.	To confirm	=	confermare	=	konfērmarē	=	कोनफिरमारे
83.	To contain	=	contenere	=	kontēnērē	=	कोनतेनेरे
84.	To control	=	controlare	=	kontrollarē	=	कोनत्रोलारे
85.	To cover	=	Coprire	=	koprirē	=	कोपरिरे
86.	To cry	=	Piangere	=	*Pianjērē*	=	प्यानजेरे
87.	To cure	=	Curare	=	kurarē	=	कूरारे
88.	To cut	=	Tagliare	=	taliarē	=	तालयारे
89.	To damage	=	danneggiare	=	danējiarē	=	दानेजारे
90.	To dance	=	Ballare	=	ballarē	=	बालआरे
91.	To dare	=	Osare	=	osarē	=	ओसारे

41

92.	To decay	=	imputridere	=	*imputridērē*	इमपुत्रीदीरे
93.	To decide	=	decidere	=	*dēcidērē*	देचीदेरे
94.	To declare	=	dichiarare	=	*dikiārarē*	देक्यारारे
95.	To defend	=	Defferire	=	*dēfferirē*	दीफेरीरे
96.	To dehydrate	=	disidratarsi	=	*dizidratarsi*	दीजीद्रातार्सी
97.	To delay	=	ritardare	=	*ritardarē*	रीतार्दारे
98.	To deliver	=	distribuire	=	*distribuirē*	दीसत्रीब्यूरे
99.	To demand	=	richiedere	=	*rikiēdērē*	रीक्येदेरे
100.	To demolish	=	demolire	=	*dēmolirē*	देमोलीरे
101.	To depart	=	partire	=	*partirē*	पारतीरे
102.	To describe	=	descrivere	=	*dēscrivērē*	देसक्रीवेरे
103.	To desire	=	volere	=	*volērē*	वोलेरे
104.	To die	=	morire	=	*morirē*	मोरीरे

105.	To dig	=	scavare	= *skavarē*	= साकावारे
106.	To dip	=	tuffarsi	= *tuffarsi*	= तुफ़ारसी
107.	To disagree	=	non essere d'accordo	= *non ēssērē*	= नान एसेरे
108.	To discolour	=	scolorirsi	= *skolarirsi*	= सकोलारिर्सी
109.	To disinfect	=	disinfettare	= *disinfettare*	= दीसइन्फेत्तारे
110.	To dislike	=	dis piacere	= *dis piacērē*	= दिसपीयाचेरे
111.	To display	=	mostrare	= *mostrarē*	= मोसत्रारे
112.	To distribute	=	distribuire	= *distriburē*	= दीसत्रीब्यूरे
113.	To do	=	fare	= *farē*	= फारे
114.	To donate	=	donare	= *donarē*	= दोनारे
115.	To dream	=	sonare	= *sonarē*	= सोनारे
116.	To drink	=	bere	= *bērē*	= बेरे

43

117.	To dribble	=	dribblare	=	*dribblarē*	=	दिरब्लारे
118.	To drop	=	goccia.	=	*Goccià*	=	गोचा
119.	To dry	=	asciugarsi	=	*asciugarsi*	=	असीगारसी
120.	To dye	=	tingersi	=	*teenjērsi*	=	तीनजेरसी
121.	To eat	=	mangiare	=	*Manjarē*	=	मानजारे
122.	To educate	=	istruire	=	*istruirē*	=	इस्त्रुइरे
123.	To elect	=	eleggere	=	*ēlēggērē*	=	एलेगेरे
124.	To embarrass	=	imbarazzare	=	*imbaratsarē*	=	इम्बरतसारे
125.	To emigrate	=	emigrare	=	*ēmigrarē*	=	इमीगारारे
126.	To encourage	=	incoraggiare	=	*inkorajiarē*	=	इनकोरजारे
127.	To enjoy	=	godere	=	*godērē*	=	गोदेरे
128.	To enter	=	entrare	=	*ēntrarē*	=	एनत्रारे
129.	To erase	=	cancellare	=	*kancēllarē*	=	कानचेलारे

44

130.	To err	=	errare	=	$\bar{e}rrar\bar{e}$	=	एरारे
131.	To escape	=	fuoriuscire	=	$fuoriuscir\bar{e}$	=	फोरिउसिरे
132.	To exhibit	=	esporre	=	$\bar{e}sporr\bar{e}$	=	एस्पोरे
133.	To expedite	=	accellerare	=	$acc\bar{e}ll\bar{e}rar\bar{e}$	=	आचीलारे
134.	To fail	=	bocciare	=	$bocciar\bar{e}$	=	बुचारे
135.	To faint	=	svenire	=	$sv\bar{e}nir\bar{e}$	=	ज्वेनीरे
136.	To fall	=	cadere	=	$kad\bar{e}r\bar{e}$	=	कादेरे
137.	To fasten	=	fissarsi	=	$fissarsi$	=	फिसारसी
138.	To fear	=	temere	=	$t\bar{e}m\bar{e}r\bar{e}$	=	तेमेरे
139.	To feed	=	allattare	=	$allattar\bar{e}$	=	अलातारे
140.	To fight	=	combattere	=	$kombatt\bar{e}r\bar{e}$	=	कोम्बातेरे
141.	To filter	=	filtrare	=	$filtrar\bar{e}$	=	फिलतरारे
142.	To finish	=	finire	=	$finire$	=	फिनीरे

45

143.	To flee	=	fuggire	=	fuggirē	= फज़िरे
144.	To flow	=	fluire	=	floirē	= फ्लुइरे
145.	To fly	=	volare	=	volarē	= वोलारे
146.	To forfeit	=	Perdere	=	pērdērē	= पेरदेरे
147.	To forget	=	dimenticarsi	=	dimēntikarsi	= दीमेन्तीकारसी
148.	To forgive	=	perdonare	=	pērdonarē	= पेरदोनारे
149.	To frighten	=	spaventare	=	spavēntarē	= स्पावेनतारे
150.	To gamble	=	Azzardo, rischio	=	Azzārdo, riskio	= अज़ारदो, रिस्कीओ
151.	To get	=	Prendere	=	Prēndērē	= प्रेनदेरे
152.	To go	=	Andare	=	Andarē	= अनदारे
153.	To guard	=	guardare	=	guardarē	= गुआरदारे
154.	To guide	=	Guidare	=	guidarē	= गुइदारे

46

155.	To hang	=	Appendare;	=	*Appēndarē*	=	अपेन्दारे
156.	To harm	=	danneggiare	=	*Dannējiare*	=	दान्नेजारे
157.	To heat	=	Ardore;	=	*Ardorē*	=	आर्दोरे
158.	To help	=	Aiutare	=	*Aiutarē*	=	आयुतारे
159.	To hesitate	=	Esitare	=	*Ēsitarē*	=	एसीतारे
160.	To hide	=	nascondere	=	*naskondērē*	=	नास्कोन्देरे
161.	To hit	=	Colpire	=	*kolpirē*	=	कोल्पिरे
162.	To hold	=	Tenere;	=	*tēnērē*	=	तेनेरे
163.	To honour	=	Onorare	=	*onorarē*	=	ओनोरारे
164.	To hug	=	abbracciare	=	*abbracciare*	=	अब्राचारे
165.	To hurt	=	Ferire	=	*Fērirē*	=	फेरीरे
166.	To hypnotise	=	ipnotizzare	=	*ipnotijarē*	=	इप्नोतीजारे
167.	To identify	=	identificare	=	*idēntifikarē*	=	इदेन्तीफिकारे

47

168.	To ignore	=	ignorare	=	ignorare	=	इग्नोरारे
169.	To imagine	=	Immaginare	=	immaginarē	=	इमाजीनारे
170.	To import	=	importare	=	importarē	=	इम्पुरतारे
171.	To improve	=	migliorare	=	miliorarē	=	मील्योरारे
172.	To include	=	includere	=	inkludērē	=	इनक्लुदेरे
173.	To indicate	=	indicare	=	indikarē	=	इन्दीकारे
174.	To influence	=	influenzare	=	influēntsarē	=	इन्फ्लुएन्त्सारे
175.	To insist	=	insistere	=	insistērē	=	इन्सीसतेरे
176.	To insure	=	assicurare	=	assikurarē	=	अस्सीकुरारे
177.	To interrupt	=	Interrompere;	=	Intērrompērē	=	इन्तेररोम्पेरे
178.	To intimate	=	Intimo	=	Intimo	=	इन्तीमो
179.	To introduce	=	presentare	=	prēsēntarē	=	प्रेजेनतारे
180.	To irrigate	=	irrigare	=	irrigarē	=	इरीगारे

48

181.	To join	=	Unire	=	*Unirē*	=	उनिरे
182.	To joke	=	Scherzare	=	*skērtsarē*	=	स्केतजारे
183.	To judge	=	Giudicare	=	*Jiudikarē*	=	जुदिकारे
184.	To jump	=	Saltare	=	*saltarē*	=	सालतारे
185.	To keep	=	Tenere	=	*Tēnē*	=	तेनेरे
186.	To kiss	=	Baciare	=	*Baciarē*	=	बाचारे
187.	To kneel	=	inginocchiarsi	=	*inginokiarsi*	=	इनजीनोकियार्सी
188.	To knock	=	Bussare	=	*Buzarē*	=	बुज्जारे
189.	To know	=	Sapere	=	*sapērē*	=	सापेरे
190.	To lack	=	mancare	=	*mankarē*	=	मानकारे
191.	To land	=	sbarkare	=	*sbarkarē*	=	स्बकारे
192.	To laugh	=	Ridere	=	*ridērē*	=	रीदेरे
193.	To lay	=	Posare	=	*posarē*	=	पोजारे

49

194.	To lead	=	condurre	=	*kondurrē*	=	कोन्दुररे
195.	To leak	=	divulgare	=	*divulgarē*	=	दीवुलगारे
196.	To leap	=	Saltare	=	*Saltarē*	=	सालतारे
197.	To leave	=	Lasciare;	=	*lasciarē*	=	लासारे
198.	To lecture	=	conferenza	=	*konfērēntsa*	=	कोन्फरेन्जा
199.	To lend	=	prestare	=	*prēstarē*	=	प्रेसतारे
200.	To lift	=	sollevare	=	*sollēvarē*	=	सोलेवारे
201.	To like	=	piacere	=	*piacērē*	=	पियाचेरे
202.	To live	=	Vivere	=	*vivērē*	=	वीवेरे
203.	To look	=	guardare	=	*guardarē*	=	गुआरदारे
204.	To loosen	=	senza stringere	=	*senza strinjērē*	=	सेन्जा स्त्रीनजेरे
205.	To love	=	Amare	=	*amarē*	=	आमारे
206.	To lubricate	=	Lubrificare	=	*lubrifikarē*	=	लुब्रीफिकारे

50

207.	To mail	=	Spedire	=	spēdirē	=	स्पेदिरे
208.	To make	=	Fare	=	farē	=	फारे
209.	To marry	=	Sposare	=	spozarē	=	स्पोजारे
210.	To mash	=	Passare	=	passarē	=	पासारे
211.	To massage	=	Mandare	=	Mandarē	=	मान्दारे
212.	To measure	=	Misurare	=	misurarē	=	मिसुरारे
213.	To meet	=	Incontrare	=	inkontrarē	=	इन्कोन्तरारे
214.	To misguide	=	guidare falso	=	guidarē falso	=	गवीदारे फाल्सो
215.	To miss	=	Perdere	=	pērdērē	=	पेरदेरे
216.	To misunderstand	=	Capire male	=	kapirē Malē	=	कापिरे माले
217.	To mix	=	Mescolare	=	Meskolarē	=	मेस्कुलारे
218.	To nag	=	Tormentare	=	Tormēntarē	=	तोरमेन्तारे

51

219.	To nap	=	Pisolino	=	*pisolino*	=	पिजोलिनो
220.	To need	=	avere Bisogno	=	*avērē Bisono*	=	आवेरे बिजोनिया
221.	To notify	=	Far sapere	=	*Far sapērē*	=	फार सापेरे
222.	To obey	=	Ubbidire	=	*ubbidirē*	=	उब्बिदिरे
223.	To observe	=	Osservare	=	*Ossērvarē*	=	ओस्सीरवारे
224.	To obtain	=	Ottenere	=	*ottēnērē*	=	आतेनेरे
225.	To occupy	=	Occupare	=	*okuparē*	=	अक्कुपारे
226.	To offer	=	Offrire	=	*offrirē*	=	ओफ्फरेरे
227.	To ooze	=	Stillare	=	*stillarē*	=	स्तिल्लारे
228.	To open	=	Aprire	=	*aprirē*	=	आप्रीरे
229.	To order	=	Ordinare	=	*ordinarē*	=	ओरदीनारे
230.	To organize	=	Organizzare	=	*organitsarē*	=	ओरगानित्सारे
231.	To overflow	=	traboccare	=	*Trabokarē*	=	त्राबोकारे

52

232.	To overload	=	Sovraccaricare	=	sovrakarikarē	=	सोवराकारीकारे
233.	To overtake	=	Sorpassare	=	sorpassarē	=	सुरपासारे
234.	To own	=	Possedere	=	possēdērē	=	पोसेदेरे
235.	To pacify	=	Calmare	=	kalmarē	=	कालमारे
236.	To paint	=	Vernicare	=	Vērnikarē	=	वेरनीकारे
237.	To pass	=	Passare	=	Passarē	=	पासारे
238.	To pay	=	Pagare	=	Pagarē	=	पागारे
239.	To peal	=	Scappare	=	skapparē	=	स्कापारे
240.	To persuade	=	Persuadere	=	Pērsuadērē	=	परसुदेरे
241.	To play	=	Giocare	=	jiokare	=	जुकारे
242.	To plead	=	Patrocinare	=	Patrocinarē	=	पेत्रोचीनारे
243.	To popularize	=	Popolare	=	Popolarē	=	पोपुलारे
244.	To post pone	=	Rinviare	=	Rinviarē	=	रीनवीयारे

53

245.	To practise	= Practicare	= pratikarē	= प्रातिकारे
246.	To pray	= Pregare	= prēgarē	= प्रेगारे
247.	To prepare	= Preparare	= Prēpararē	= प्रेपारारे
248.	To pressurize	= Forzare	= Fortsarē	= फुरत्सारे
249.	To prevent	= Impediare a qualcuno di fare	= Impēdiarē a qualcuno di larē	= इम्पेदीयारे आ क्वालकुनो दी फारे
250.	To prick	= Pungere	= Punjērē	= पुन्जेरे
251.	To produce	= Prodotto	= Produrrē	= प्रेदुर्रे
252.	To prolong	= Prolungare	= Prolungarē	= प्रोलुंगारे
253.	To prove	= Provare	= Provarē	= प्रोवारे
254.	To provoke	= Provocare	= Provokarē	= प्रोवोकारे
255.	To punish	= Punire	= Punirē	= पुनीरे

54

256.	To purchase	=	Comprare	=	*Komprarē*	=	कोम्प्ररे
257.	To push	=	Spingere	=	*Spinjērē*	=	स्पिन्जरे
258.	To qualify	=	Abilitare	=	*Abilitarē*	=	अबीलीतारे
259.	To quarrel	=	Litigare	=	*litigarē*	=	लितीगारे
260.	To question	=	Domandare	=	*Domandarē*	=	दोमान्दारे
261.	To quit	=	Mollare	=	*Mollarē*	=	मोल्लारे
262.	To rain	=	Piovere	=	*piovērē*	=	प्योवेरे
263.	To reach	=	Arrivare	=	*arrivarē*	=	अरीवारे
264.	To read	=	Leggere	=	*lejērē*	=	लेजीरे
265.	To recommend	=	Raccomandare	=	*Rakomandarē*	=	राकोम्मान्दारे
266.	To reduce	=	Ridurre	=	*ridurrē*	=	रीदुर्रे
267.	To regret	=	Rimpiangere	=	*Rimpianjērē*	=	रीम्प्यान्जेरे

55

268.	To reject	=	Rifiutare	=	रिफ्युतारे
269.	To relax	=	Rilasciarsi	=	रीलासारसी
270.	To relieve	=	Sollevare	=	सोलेवारे
271.	To repair	=	Riparare	=	रीपारारे
272.	To repeat	=	Ripetere	=	रीपेतेरे
273.	To reply	=	Rispondere	=	रीसपोन्दरे
274.	To report	=	Rapportare	=	रापोरतारे
275.	To rescue	=	Salvare	=	सालवारे
276.	To rest	=	Riposare	=	रीपोसारे
277.	To return	=	Ritornare	=	रीतोरनारे
278.	To ride	=	Cavalcare	=	कावालकारे
279.	To rise	=	Alzarsi	=	अलजारसी
280.	To roar	=	Ruggire	=	रूजीरे

56

281.	To roast	=	Arrostire	= *Arrostirē*	= आरोस्तिरे
282.	To rub	=	Strofinare	= *Strofinarē*	= स्त्रोफिनारे
283.	To run	=	Correre	= *korrērē*	= कोरेरे
284.	To rush	=	Mandare Velociamente	= *Mandarē Velociamēnte*	= मान्दारे वेलोचामेन्ते
285.	To sacrifice	=	Sacrificare	= *Sakrifikarē*	= सेक्रीफिकारे
286.	To sanction	=	Sanznare	= *santsionarē*	= सान्त्सीयोनारे
287.	To satisfy	=	Soddisfare	= *soddisfarē*	= सोदीसफारे
288.	To save	=	Salvare	= *salvarē*	= सालवारे
289.	To say	=	Dire	= *dirē*	= दिरे
290.	To scatter	=	Spargere	= *Sparjērē*	= स्पारजेरे
291.	To scratch	=	Graffire	= *Graffirē*	= ग्राफिरे
292.	To scream	=	Gridare	= *Gridarē*	= ग्रीदारे

293.	To search	=	Cercare	=	Cērkarē	=	चेरकारे
294.	To see	=	Vedere	=	vēdērē	=	वेदेरे
295.	To seek	=	Cercare	=	cerkaré	=	चेरकारे
296.	To sell	=	Vendere	=	vēndērē	=	वेनदेरे
297.	To select	=	Scegliere	=	scēliērē	=	सेल्यीरे
298.	To separate	=	Separare	=	Sēpararē	=	सेपारारे
299.	To shake	=	Scuotere	=	Skuotērē	=	स्कोतेरे
300.	To share	=	Dividere	=	dividerē	=	दीवीदारे
301.	To shatter	=	Frantumare	=	Frantumarē	=	फ्रान्तुमारे
302.	To shrink	=	Restringersi	=	Rēstrinjērsi	=	रेस्त्रीनजेरसी
303.	To shut	=	Chiudersi	=	kiudērsi	=	क्योदेरसी
304.	To sing	=	Cantare	=	Kantarē	=	कानतारे
305.	To sink	=	Affondare	=	Affondarē	=	अफोनदारे

58

306.	To sit	= Sedere	= Sēdēre	= सेदेरे
307.	To slip	= Scivolare	= Scivolarē	= सीवोलारे
308.	To smell	= Odore	= Odorē	= ओदोरे
309.	To snatch	= Strappare	= strapparē	= स्त्रापारे
310.	To speak	= Parlare	= parlarē	= पारलारे
311.	To spit	= sputare	= sputarē	= स्पुतारे
312.	To spoil	= Rovinare	= rovinarē	= रोवीनारे
313.	To spray	= spruzzare	= sprutsare	= स्पुत्सारे
314.	To spread	= distendere	= distēndērē	= दीसतेन्देरे
315.	To stab	= Pugnalata;	= Punalarē	= पुनलारे
316.	To stain	= maccihare	= Makiharē	= माकयारे
317.	To stand	= stare in piedi	= starē in Piēdi	= स्तारे इन पीयेदी

59

318.	To stare	= Fissare	= Fissarē	= फिस्सारे
319.	To start	= iniziare	= Initsiarē	= इनीतसयारे
320.	To stay	= stare	= starē	= स्तारे
321.	To steal	= Rubare	= rubarē	= रूबारे
322.	To stop	= fermare	= Fērmarē	= फरमारे
323.	To store	= conservare	= Consērvarē	= कोन्जरवारे
324.	To stretch	= Stirarsi	= stirarsi	= स्तीरारसी
325.	To suck	= Succhiare	= sukiarē	= सूक्यारे
326.	To suffer	= Soffirire	= soffirirē	= सोफीरीरे
327.	To surprise	= sorprendere	= sorprēndērē	= सोरप्रेनदेरे
328.	To surrender	= Arrendersi	= arrēndērsi	= अरेन्देरसी
329.	To swell	= Gonfiare	= Gonfiarē	= गोनफ्यारे
330.	To tackle	= affrontare	= affrontarē	= आफ्रोनतारे

60

331.	To tag	=	*sēguirē*	=	सेगविरे
332.	To take	=	*Prēndērē*	=	प्रेन्देरे
333.	To talk	=	*parlarē*	=	पारलारे
334.	To tap	=	*struttarē*	=	स्त्रुतारे
335.	To tape	=	*rēgistrarē*	=	रेजिस्त्रारे
336.	To tattoo	=	*Tatuarē*	=	ताठुआरे
337.	To teach	=	*Insēnarē*	=	इन्सेन्आरे
338.	To tear	=	*Strapparsi*	=	स्त्रापारसी
339.	To testify	=	*tēstimoniarē*	=	तेस्तीमुन्यारे
340.	To thank	=	*Ringratsiarē*	=	रीगरात्सीआरे
341.	To think	=	*Pēnsarē*	=	पेन्सारे
342.	To throw	=	*lanciarē*	=	लांचारे

61

343.	To tie	=	Annodare	= *annodarē*	= अनुदारे
344.	To tolerate	=	Sopportare	= *sopportarē*	= स्पोरतारे
345.	To torture	=	Torturare	= *Torturarē*	= तोरतुरारे
346.	To touch	=	Toccare	= *Tokarē*	= तुकारे
347.	To translate	=	Tradurre	= *Tradurrē*	= त्राडुर्रे
348.	To tremble	=	Tremare	= *Trēmarē*	= त्रेमारे
349.	To trim	=	Spuntare	= *spontarē*	= स्पुनतारे
350.	To trust	=	Fidare	= *Fidare*	= फिदारे
351.	To try	=	Provare	= *Provarē*	= प्रोवारे
352.	To turn	=	Girare	= *Jirarē*	= जिरारे
353.	To type	=	Genere	= *Jēnērē*	= जेनेरे
354.	To understand	=	Capire	= *Kapirē*	= कापिरे
355.	To undress	=	Spogliarsi	= *Spoliarsi*	= स्पोलेआरसी

62

356.	To unite	=	Unire	=	Unirē	=	उनीरे
357.	To unload	=	Scaricare	=	Skarikarē	=	स्कारीकारे
358.	To unlock	=	Aprire	=	Aprirē	=	आपरीरे
359.	To upset	=	Contrattempo	=	kontrattēmpo	=	कोन्त्रातेम्पु
360.	To use	=	Usare	=	Usarē	=	उसारे
361.	To vacate	=	Lasciare libero	=	Lasciarē libēro	=	लासारे लिबेरो
362.	To vary	=	Variare	=	Variarē	=	वारीआरे
363.	To violate	=	Violare	=	Violarē	=	वियोलारे
364.	To vote	=	Votare	=	Votarē	=	वुतारे
365.	To wait	=	Aspettare	=	Aspēttarē	=	अस्पेतारे
366.	To wake	=	Svegliare	=	Sveliarē	=	स्वेलीआरे
367.	To walk	=	Scamminare	=	Kaminarē	=	कामीनारे

63

368.	To wander	=	Girare senza meta	=	Girarē Sēnzā mēta	=	जिरारे सेन्जा मेता
369.	To warm	=	Scaldare	=	Skaldarē	=	स्कालदारे
370.	To wash	=	Lavare	=	Lavarē	=	लावारे
371.	To waste	=	Sprecare	=	sprē Karē	=	स्प्रेकारे
372.	To watch	=	Guardare	=	Guardarē	=	गुआरदारे
373.	To wave	=	Sventolare	=	Svēntolarē	=	ज्वेन्तोलारे
374.	To weigh	=	Pesare	=	pēsarē	=	पेजारे
375.	To whip	=	Frustare	=	Frustarē	=	फ्रुसतारे
376.	To whisper	=	Sussurrare	=	sussurrarē	=	सुसुरारे
377.	To whistle	=	Fischiare	=	Fisciārē	=	फिस्सारे
378.	To wink	=	Ammiccare	=	Ammikarē	=	आम्मिकारे
379.	To withdraw	=	Ritirare	=	Ritirarē	=	रीतीरारे

380.	To work	=	Lavorare	=	लावोरारे
381.	To worry	=	preoccupare	=	प्रीओक्कुपारे
382.	To write	=	scrivere	=	स्क्रीवेरे

Lavorarē

prēōkuparē

skrivērē

65

Nouns

	English		Italian		Hindi
1.	Account	=	Cliente	= *Kontō*	= कोन्तो
2.	Acid	=	Acido	= *Acidoo*	= अचीदो
3.	Actor	=	Attore	= *attore*	= अत्तोरे
4.	Address	=	Indirizzo	= *Indiritso*	= इन्दिरत्सो
5.	Advertisement	=	Pubblicità	= *pubbli-Città*	= पुब्ली चिता
6.	Agriculture	=	Agricoltura	= *Agri-coltura*	= आग्री कूलतुरा
7.	Anger	=	Rabbia	= *Rabb-ia*	= राबीया
8.	Animal	=	Animale	= *Animalē*	= अनीमाले
9.	Ankle	=	Caviglia	= *Caviglia*	= कावील्या
10.	Answer	=	Risposta	= *Risposta*	= रिसपोस्ता
11.	Apology	=	Scuse	= *Skusa*	= स्कूजा

66

#	English		Italian		Italian		Devanagari
12.	Arch	=	Arco	=	*Arco*	=	आरको
13.	Arm	=	Braccio	=	*Bra-ccio*	=	ब्राचो
14.	Armpit	=	Asella	=	*Asélla*	=	असेला
15.	Baby	=	Bambino	=	*Bombino*	=	बाम्बीनो
16.	Bachelor	=	Scapolo	=	*Skapolo*	=	स्कापोलो
17.	Back	=	Parte posteriore	=	*Partē Postēriarē*	=	पार्टे पोसतेरिओरे
18.	Backbone	=	Base	=	*Spina Dorsalē*	=	स्पीना दोरसाले
19.	Backyard	=	Cortile	=	*Cortilē*	=	कोरतीले
20.	Banana	=	Banana	=	*Banana*	=	बनाना
21.	Beard	=	Barba	=	*Barbā*	=	बारबा
22.	Bed	=	Letto	=	*Letto*	=	लेतो
23.	Blister	=	Bolla	=	*Bolla*	=	बुला
24.	Blood	=	Sangue	=	*sanvē*	=	सान्वे
25.	Belly	=	Pancia	=	*pancia*	=	पान्चा
26.	Book	=	Libro	=	*libro*	=	लिब्रो

27.	Boy	Ragazzo	= ragatso	= रागात्सो
28.	Brain	Cervello	= cer-vello	= चेरवेलो
29.	Bride	Bride	= spo-sā	= स्पोजा
30.	Bug	Insetto	= insētto	= इन्सेत्तो
31.	Butter	Burro	= Burro	= बुरो
32.	Cabbage	Cavolo	= kavolo	= कवालो
33.	Calf	Vitello	= vitēllo	= वितेलो
34.	Camel	Cammello	= kammello	= कम्मेलो
35.	Cap	Capello	= kapēllo	= कापेलो
36.	Carpet	Moquette	= Moquēttē	= मुकेते
37.	Carrot	Carota	= corotā	= कारोता
38.	Chair	Sedia	= sēdia	= सेदीया
39.	Chameleon	Chameleon	= chamēlēon	= केमेलियन
40.	Cheek	Guancica	= Guan-cia	= गवान्चा
41.	Chest	Cassa	= ka-ssa	= कास्सा

68

42.	Citizen	=	Cittadino	= *Chitta-dino*	= चित्तादीनो
43.	Coal	=	Carbone	= *karbonē*	= कारबोने
44.	Coast	=	Coasta	= *coasta*	= कोसता
45.	Coin	=	Moneta	= *monēta*	= मुन्ता
46.	Colour	=	Colore	= *Colorē*	= कोलोरे
47.	Corner	=	Angolo	= *Ang-golo*	= आनगोलो
48.	Coward	=	Vigliacco	= *Viliacco*	= वीलाचो
49.	Cow	=	Mucca	= *Muka*	= मुक्का
50.	Crime	=	Crimine	= *Criminē*	= क्रिमिने
51.	Crop	=	Il raccolto	= *ll rakcolto*	= राकोलतो
52.	Crow	=	Corvo	= *korvo*	= कोरवो
53.	Crown	=	Parte superiore	= *partē*	= पारते
54.	Custody	=	Custodia	= *kustodiā*	= कुसतुदीया
55.	Dance	=	Ballo	= *Ballo*	= बालो
56.	Danger	=	Pericolo	= *Pērikolo*	= पेरीकोलो

69

57.	Date	= Data	= *data*	= दाता
58.	Day	= Giorno	= *gior-no*	= जोरनो
59.	Death	= Morte	= *Mortē*	= मारते
60.	Decoration	= Decorazione	= *Dēkortsionē*	= देकोरात्सियोने
61.	Deer	= Cervi	= *Cērvi*	= चेर्वी
62.	Department	= Reparto	= *Rēparto*	= रेपारतो
63.	Desert	= Deserto	= *Dēsērto*	= देजेरतो
64.	Dog	= Cane	= *kanē*	= कानं
65.	Door	= Portello	= *portēllo*	= पोरतेलो
66.	Doubt	= Dubbio	= *dubbio*	= दुब्यो
67.	Dozen	= Dozzina	= *Dotsina*	= दोतसीना
68.	Dream	= Sogno	= *so-ono*	= सोनो
69.	Dress	= Vestito	= *Vēstito*	= वेसतीतो
70.	Drink	= Bevanda	= *Bēvanda*	= बेवान्दा
71.	Drop	= Goccia	= *Go-ccia*	= गोचा

72.	Duck	=	Anatra	= *Anatrē*	= अनात्रा
73.	Dump	=	Deposito	= *Dēposito*	= देपोजितो
74.	Dust	=	Polvere	= *polvērē*	= पोल्वेरे
75.	Eagle	=	Aquila	= *Akuila*	= अक्वीला
76.	Ear	=	Orecchio	= *orēdcio*	= ओरेक्यु
77.	Earth	=	Terra	= *Tērra*	= तेरा
78.	East	=	Orientale	= *Oriēntalē*	= ओरीयेन्ताले
79.	Echo	=	Eco	= *Ēco*	= एको
80.	Economy	=	Economia	= *Ēconomia*	= एकोनोमिया
81.	Editor	=	Redattore	= *Rēdattorē*	= रेदातोरे
82.	Education	=	Formazione	= *Formazionē*	= फोरमात्सिओने
83.	Eclipse	=	Eclissi	= *Eklissi*	= एकलीसी
84.	Elbow	=	Gomito	= *Gomito*	= गोमीतो
85.	End	=	Estremità	= *Estrēmita*	= एस्त्रेमिता
86.	Energy	=	Energia	= *Enērgia*	= एनेर्जिया

71

	English		Italian		Devanagari
87.	Environment	=	Ambiēnte	=	आम्बीएन्ते
88.	Event	=	Evēnto	=	इवेन्तो
89.	Eye	=	Okio	=	ओक्यो
90.	Eye brow	=	Sopracilio	=	सोप्राचिल्यो
91.	Eye lashes	=	Sfērze dellokio	=	स्फेर्जे देल्लओक्यो
92.	Eye witness	=	Tēstimonēdēllokio	=	तेस्तीमुन देल्लओक्यो
93.	Face	=	Facciā	=	फाच्चा
94.	Fair	=	Giusto	=	जुस्तो
95.	Fan	=	Vēntilatorē	=	वेन्तीलातोरे
96.	Farm	=	Podērē	=	पोदेरे
97.	Father	=	Padrē	=	पाद्रे
98.	Fire	=	Fuoko	=	फुओको
99.	Finger	=	Barrētta	=	बारेत्ता
100.	Fish	=	Pēsci	=	पेसी

101. Flag	=	Bandierina	=	बान्देरीना
102. Flame	=	Fiamma	=	फियाम्मा
103. Flesh	=	Carnē	=	कारने
104. Fly	=	Mosca	=	मोस्का
105. Floor	=	Pavimēnto	=	पावीमेन्तो
106. Flour	=	Farinā	=	फरीना
107. Flower	=	Fiorē	=	फियोरे
108. Flower pot	=	Vaso delliovē	=	वासुदेल फियोरे
109. Flute	=	Skanalatura	=	स्कानालातुरा
110. Foam	=	Go-mma pewma	=	गोम्माप्युमा
111. Fog	=	Nēbbia	=	नेब्या
112. Foot	=	Piēdē	=	पीयेदे
113. Forehead	=	Frontē	=	फ्रोन्ते
114. Fort	=	Fortē	=	फोरते
115. Fountain	=	Fontana	=	फोन्ताना

73

116. Frog	=	Rana	=	Rana	रानl
117. Fuel	=	Combustibile	=	Combustibilē	कुम्बुसतीबीलॆ
118. Function	=	Funzione	=	Funtsionē	फुनसीओनॆ
119. Future	=	Futuro	=	Futuro	फुतुरो
120. Gamble	=	Gioco	=	Gio-co	जोको
121. Garbage	=	Immondizia	=	Immondizia	इम्मोनदिज़िया
122. Garden	=	Giardino	=	Gar-dino	जारदीनो
123. Girl	=	Ragazza	=	Ragaisa	रागात्सा
124. Glass	=	Vetro	=	vētro	वॆतरो
125. Glove	=	Guanto	=	Guanto	गुआनतो
126. Glue	=	Colla	=	Colla	कोला
127. Goat	=	Capra	=	Kapra	कापरा
128. God	=	Dio	=	Dio	दीयो
129. Gold	=	Oro	=	Oro	ओरो
130. Grand father	=	Nonno	=	Grandē Padrē	नोन्नो

74

131. Grand mother	=	Nonna	=	*Grandē madrē*	=	नोना
132. Grape	=	Uva	=	*Uva*	=	उआ
133. Grave	=	Tomba	=	*Tomba*	=	तोम्बा
134. Guard	=	Protezione	=	*protetsionē*	=	प्रोतेतसीओने
135. Guest	=	Ospite	=	*ospitē*	=	ओस्पीते
136. Gum	=	Gomma	=	*Gomma*	=	गोम्मा
137. Habit	=	Abitudine	=	*Abitudinē*	=	अबीतुदीने
138. Hair	=	Capelli	=	*capēlli*	=	कापेली
140. Hand	=	Mano	=	*Mano*	=	मानो
141. Hammer	=	Martello	=	*martēllo*	=	मारतेलो
142. Hazard	=	Rischio	=	*Riskio*	=	रीसकियो
143. Head	=	Testa	=	*Tēsta*	=	तेसता
144. Heap	=	Mucchio	=	*Mukio*	=	मुक्कियो
145. Heart	=	Cuore	=	*kuorē*	=	कोरे

75

146. Heat	=	Calore	= calorē	= कालोरे
147. Heel	=	Tallone	= Tallonē	= तालोने
148. Hip	=	Anca	= anka	= आन्का
149. History	=	Storia	= storia	= स्तोरिया
150. Hole	=	Foro.	= Foro	= फ़ुरो
151. Home	=	Domestico	= Domēstiko	= दोमेस्तिको
152. Honey	=	Miele	= miēlē	= मिय़ेले
153. Horn	=	Corno	= korno	= कोरनो
154. Horse	=	Cavallo	= kavallo	= कावालो
155. Hour	=	Ora	= ora	= ओरा
156. Husband	=	Marito	= Marito	= मारीतो
157. Hypnosis	=	Ipnosi	= ipnosi	= इप्नोसी
158. Importance	=	Importanza	= importanza	= इम्पोरतान्जा
159. Industrial	=	Industriale	= Industrealē	= इन्दुस्त्रियाले

76

	Information	=	Le informazioni	=	Le Informatsioni	=	ले
160.	Information	=		=		=	इन्फोर्मात्सियोने
161.	Jewellery	=	Monili	=	Monili	=	मोनीली
162.	Joke	=	Scherzo	=	sketso	=	स्केतसो
163.	Judgment	=	Giudizio	=	Gioditsio	=	जुदीतसिओ
164.	Key	=	Chiave	=	Kiavē	=	कियावे
165.	Knife	=	coltello	=	koltēllo	=	कोलतेलो
166.	Knot	=	Nodo	=	Nōdoo	=	नोदो
167.	Knee	=	Ginocchio	=	jenokeeyoo	=	जिनोकियो
168.	Knowledge	=	Conoscenza	=	konosenza	=	कोनोसेन्ज़ा
169.	Laboratory	=	Laboratorio	=	laboratorio	=	लाबोरातोरियो
170.	Lad	=	Lad	=	Laad	=	लाड़
171.	Lady	=	Signora	=	sinorā	=	सीनोरा
172.	Lamb	=	Agnello	=	anēllo	=	अनेलो
173.	Land	=	Terra	=	Tērra	=	तेर्रा

174. Lane	=	stradina	=	*stradinā*	स्त्रादीना
175. Language	=	Lingua	=	*Ling-ua*	लिंगवा
176. Lap	=	Giro	=	*Giro*	जीरो
177. Laughter	=	risate	=	*Risatē*	रिसाते
178. Law	=	Legge	=	*Lēggē*	लेज्जे
179. Leaf	=	Foglio	=	*Folio*	फोलयो
180. Leather	=	Cuoio	=	*co-o-io*	कोयो
181. Leopard	=	Leopardo	=	*Lēo pardo*	लियोपारदो
182. Lemon	=	Limone	=	*Limonē*	लिमोने
183. Lettuce	=	Lattuga	=	*lattuga*	लाहुगा
184. Life	=	Vita	=	*Vita*	वीता
185. Leg	=	gamba	=	*gambā*	गाम्बा
186. Lip	=	Labbro	=	*Labbro*	लाब्बो
187. Literature	=	Letteratura	=	*lēttēratura*	लेत्तेरातुरा
188. Lock	=	Serratura	=	*Sēra tura*	सेरातुरा

78

189. Lotus	=	Loto	=	लोतो
190. Love	=	Amore	*Amo-rē*	आमोरे
191. Lover	=	Amante	*amantē*	आमान्ते
192. Lunch	=	Pranzo	*Pranso*	प्रान्जो
193. Lung	=	Polmone	*Polmonē*	पुलमोने
194. Magic	=	Magia	*ma-Ja*	माजा
195. Magnet	=	Magnete	*Magnētē*	मागनेते
196. Maid	=	Domestica	*Domēstika*	दोमेस्तिका
197. Majority	=	Maggioranza	*majorantsa*	माज्योरान्जा
198. Man	=	Uomo	*Uomo*	उओमो
199. Map	=	carta	*Karta*	कारता
200. Massage	=	Massaggio	*Mēssajo*	मेसाज्यो
201. Material	=	Materiale	*Matērialē*	मातेरिआले
202. Meal	=	Pasto	*Pasto*	पास्तो
203. Medicine	=	Medicina	*Mēdicina*	मेदीचिना

		English		Italian		Hindi
204.	Melon	=	Melone	=	*Melonē*	=	मेलोने
205.	Mind	=	Mente	=	*Mēntē*	=	मेन्ते
206.	Mirror	=	Specchio	=	*Spekio*	=	स्पेकियो
207.	Monument	=	Monumento	=	*Monumēnto*	=	मोनुमेन्तो
208.	Mosquito	=	Zanzara	=	*Zanzara*	=	जानजारा
209.	Murder	=	Omicidio	=	*omi-cidi-o*	=	आमीचीदियो
210.	Murder	=	Omicidio	=	*aameechideeyoo*	=	आमीचीदियो
211.	Mustache	=	Mustache	=	*Mustakē*	=	मूसतके
212.	Mustard	=	Senape	=	*Sēnapē*	=	सेनापे
213.	Mystery	=	Mistero	=	*Mistēro*	=	मिसतेरो
214.	Name	=	Nome	=	*Nomē*	=	नामे
215.	Nationality	=	Nazionalità	=	*Natsionalita*	=	नात्सीनालिता
216.	Nature	=	Natura	=	*natura*	=	नातुरा
217.	Need	=	Bisogno	=	*Bizonio*	=	बिजोनो
218.	Needle	=	Ago	=	*Ago*	=	आगो

80

	English		Italian				
219.	Neighbour	=	Vicino	=	*Vicino*	=	विचिनो
220.	Nest	=	Nido	=	*Nidō*	=	नीदो
221.	News	=	Notizie	=	*Noti-tsié*	=	नोतिसिया
222.	Night	=	Notte	=	*Nottē*	=	नोते
223.	Nose	=	Naso	=	*Naso*	=	नाजो
224.	Neck	=	Collo	=	*Kollo*	=	कालो
225.	Nail	=	Chiodo	=	*Kiodo*	=	कियोदो
226.	Onion	=	Cipolla	=	*chipolla*	=	चिपोला
227.	Owl	=	Gufo	=	*Gufo*	=	गुफो
228.	Pain	=	Dolore	=	*Dolorē*	=	दोलोरे
229.	Palm	=	Palma	=	*Palma*	=	पालमा
230.	Parrot	=	Pappagallo	=	*Pappa-gallo*	=	पापागालो
231.	Patient	=	Paziente	=	*Patsiēntē*	=	पातसीएन्ते
232.	Peacock	=	pavone	=	*Pavonē*	=	पावोने
233.	People	=	popolo	=	*Popolo*	=	पोपोलो

234. Pepper	=	Pepe	=	*Pēpē*	=	पेपे
235. Person	=	Persona	=	*Pērsonē*	=	पर्सोना
236. Pillow	=	Guanciale	=	*Guanciale*	=	कुचीनो
237. Place	=	Luogo	=	*Luogo*	=	लुओगो
238. Poison	=	Veleno	=	*vēlēno*	=	वेलेनो
239. Population	=	Popolazione	=	*Popolatsionē*	=	पोपुलात्सियोने
240. Pot	=	Vaso	=	*Va-zo*	=	वासो
241. Potato	=	Patata	=	*Patata*	=	पाताता
242. Prayer	=	Preghiera	=	*Preg- iĕra*	=	प्रेगयेरा
243. Price	=	Prezzo	=	*pre tsso*	=	प्रेत्सो
244. Prize	=	Premio	=	*prēmio*	=	प्रेमियो
245. Prince	=	Principe	=	*Principē*	=	प्रिन्चीपे
246. Princess	=	Principessa	=	*principessā*	=	प्रिन्चीपेसा
247. Queen	=	Regina	=	*Re-Jina*	=	रेजिना
248. Question	=	Domanda	=	*Domanda*	=	दोमान्दा

249. Rabbit	=	Coniglio	= *koni-llo*	कोनिल्लियो
250. Race	=	Corsa	= *Korsa*	कोरसा
251. Reason	=	Ragione	= *Ra-gi-one*	राजीओन
252. Refugee	=	Rifugiato	= *rifu giato*	रिफ़ुजातो
253. Residence	=	Residenza	= *Rēsidinza*	रेजिदेंनजा
254. River	=	Fiume	= *Fi-umē*	फयुमे
255. Rock	=	Roccia	= *Rokaa*	रोका
256. Roof	=	Tetto	= *Tētto*	तेत्तो
257. Root	=	Radice	= *Radicē*	रादीचे
258. Rose	=	Rosa	= *Rosa*	रोसा
259. Sacred	=	Sacro	= *Sakro*	साक्रो
260. Salary	=	Stipendio	= *Stipēn dio*	स्तीपेन्दियो
261. Salt	=	Sale	= *Salē*	साले
262. Sand	=	Sabbia	= *Sabbiā*	साब्बिया
263. Scorpion	=	Scorpion	= *scorpionkas*	स्कोरपियोन

83

	English		Italian		Hindi
264.	Season	=	Stagione	=	स्ताजिग्योने
265.	She	=	Lei	=	लेइ
266.	Sheet	=	Foglio	=	फोलियो
267.	Song	=	Canzone	=	कान्जोने
268.	Skin	=	Pelle	=	पेले
269.	Sky	=	Cielo	=	चेलो
270.	Slap	=	Schiaffo	=	स्कियाफियो
271.	Snake	=	Serpente	=	सेरपेन्ते
272.	Society	=	Società	=	सोचिता
273.	South	=	sud	=	सुद
274.	Spoon	=	Cucchiaio	=	कूकिक्याओ
275.	Thing	=	Cosa	=	कोसा
276.	Thigh	=	Coscia	=	कोसीया
277.	Thousand	=	Mille	=	मिल्ले
278.	Time	=	Tempo	=	तेम्पो

84

279. Toe	=	Punta	= *Puntā*	= पुन्ता
280. Tooth	=	Dente	= *dēntē*	= देन्ते
281. Trade	=	Commercio	= *commērcio*	= कोमेरचो
283. Umbrella	=	Ombrello	= *omb-rello*	= ओम्ब्रेलो
284. Vegetable	=	Verdura	= *vēr dura*	= वेरदुरा
285. Vehicle	=	Veicolo	= *vēikolo*	= वेयीकोलो
286. Village	=	Villaggio	= *Villa-ggio*	= विलाजो
287. Violet	=	Viola	= *viola*	= वियोला
288. Volcano	=	Vulcano	= *vulkano*	= वुलकानो
289. Waist	=	Vita	= *vita*	= विता
290. Water	=	Acqua	= *akua*	= आक्वा
291. Wave	=	Onda	= *onda*	= ओंदा
292. Wax	=	Cera	= *Cēra*	= चेरा
293. Weapon	=	Arma	= *Arma*	= आरमा
294. Week	=	Settimana	= *Sēttimana*	= सेतीमान्ना

85

295.	Weight	=	Peso	=	*pezo*	पेसो
296.	West	=	ovest	=	*ovēst*	आवेस्त
297.	Wheel	=	Ruota	=	*ru-otā*	रोओता
298.	Wind	=	Vento	=	*Vēnto*	वेन्तो
299.	Woman	=	Donna	=	*Donna*	दोन्ना
300.	Word	=	Parola	=	*Pārolā*	पारोला
301.	Work	=	Lavoro	=	*Lāvoro*	लावोरो
302.	World	=	Mondo	=	*Mondo*	मोन्दो
303.	Worship	=	Culto	=	*kulto*	कुल्तो
304.	Year	=	Anno	=	*anno*	आन्नो
305.	Yesterday	=	Ieri	=	*Iēri*	इयेरी
306.	Youth	=	Gioventù	=	*Gioventù*	जुवेन्तू

Introduce yourself

1. I am British.
   Sono britannico.
   Sono britannicoo.
   सोनो ब्रितानिको

2. But I have US citizenship.
   Ma ho cittadinanza di us.
   Ma oo cittadinantza di us.
   मा ओ चितादिनान्जा दी युस।

3. I have come from Singapore.
   Vengo da Singapore.
   Vēngo da Singapore.
   वेंगो दा सिंगापुर।

4. Oh, my name is ....
   Ho Mi chiamo................
   Oh Mi ki-amo ....
   ओ मिक्यामो।

5. I am a teacher by profession.
   Sono Insegnante da Professione.
   Sono insaynantē da profētzionē.
   सोनो इनसिनयान्ते दा प्रोफेतसियोने।

6. My hobbies are-travelling and writing.
   Miei Passatempi soni viagiare e scrivere.
   Mi-ēi Passatēmpi soni vi-agar ē scrivērē.
   मियेई पासातेमपी सोनो वियेजारे ए स्रीवेरे।

7. I have a passport valid upto ....

87

Ho passaporto valido fino.
oo passaporto vaalido fino.
ओ पासापोरतो वालिदो फिनो।

8. My visa lasts on …………..
Mio visto fine su……………..
Mio visto finy su.
मियो विस्तो फिनो सु।

9. I am married.
Sono sposoto.
Sono spoozato.
सोनो स्पोजातो।

10. No, my wife has not come with me.
No, Mia moglie non viene con me.
No, me-a mo-liey non vynē con mē.
नो मिया मोलिये नान वियने कोन मे।

11. I have come alone.
Vengo solo.
Vēngo solo.
वेंगो सोलो।

12. I have never been to this country before.
Sono mai in questa paese prima.
Sono mai in quēsta paēzē prima.
सोनो माई इन कुऐस्ता पाएजे प्रिमा।

13. Along with Mount Abu, I have to visit Jaipur also.
Insieme con mount abu, devo visitare Jaipur anche.
Inseēmē con mount abu dēvo visitare Jaipur aankay.

इनसिएमे कोन माउंट आबु देवो विजितारे जयपुर आनके।

14. I'll catch my flight back on ....
Afferrerò mio volo di nuovo su.............
Affeyrēroh mio volo di nuovo su.
आफरेरो मियो वोलो दी नुओवो सु।

15. My height is 6ft. 2inches.
Mia altezza e 6 piedi 2 pollici.
Mia altēzza e 6 peēdi 2 pollici.
मिया अलतेजा ए 6 पियेदी 2 पुलीची।

16. My weight is 82 kilograms.
Mio peso e 82 chilogrammo.
Mio pēzo e 82 kilogrammo.
मियो पेजो ए 82 किलोग्रामो।

17. I have got my suite booked at hotel Radisson.
Ho prenotato mio appartaminto a albirgo radisson.
oo Prēnotato mio appartamento ā albērgo Radisson.
ओ प्रेनोतातो मियो अपारतामेन्तो आ अलबेरगो रेडिसन।

18. I have visited almost the whole of Europe.
Ho visitato quasi tutta la europa.
Oo visitato quasi tutta la europa.
ओ विजितातो कुआजी तुत्ता ला युरोपा।

19. I find hospitality of Indians really great.
Trovo ospitalita di indiani veramente grandi.
Troovo ospitalitā di indiani vēramēn tē granday.
त्रोवो ओसपितालिता दी इनदयानी वेरामेन्ते ग्रान्दे।

20. I prefer vegetarian food.

Prefrisco il cibo vegetariano.
Prēfrisco il cibo Vēgētariano.
प्रेफिस्को इल चीबो वेजेत्रयानो।

21. I have a good camera.
Ho una macchina Fotografica buona.
Oo una macchina fotografika buona.
ओ उना माकिना फोतोग्राफिका बुअना।

22. My luggage is light and simple.
Mio bagagli e leggero e semplice.
Mio bagaali ā lējēro a sēmpleecē.
मियो बागाली आ लेजेरो आ सेमप्लीचे।

23. I have not brought my laptop computer.
Non porto mio laptop.
Non porto mio laaptop.
नान पोरतो मियो लापतोप।

24. I will take some books with me.
Porterò alcuni libri con me.
Portēroo alcuni libri con mē.
पोरतेरो अलकुनी लिबरी कोन मे।

25. I can give you this book free.
Posso darti questo libro libero.
Po-sso daarti quēsto libro libēro.
पोसो दारती कुएस्तो लिबरो लिबेरो।

Introduce at the customs

1. Do I have to fill up any paper?
   Io devo compilare dei fogli ?
   Io dēvo compilare dei foli?
   इओ देवो कोमपीलारे देई फोली?

2. Where do I sign?
   Dove firmo?
   dovē firmo?
   दोवे फिरमो?

3. Yes, both these black bags are mine!
   Si, Tutte edue queste nere borse sono miep.
   See tutte e dooè questē nērē borse sono mie.
   सी तुत्ते ए दुए कुएस्ते नेरे बोरसे सोनो मिये।

4. No, that leather suitcase is not mine.
   No questa cuoio valigia non è mia.
   No questa cooio valiga non ē mia.
   नो कुएस्ता कुऐओ वालीज्या नान ए मिया।

5. What do I have to declare?
   Cosa devo dichiarare?
   Coza devo dichierarē?
   कोजा देवो दिक्येरारे?

6. Is this bottle of perfume dutiable?
   E questa bottiglia di profumo dutiable?
   Ē quēsta bottilia di profumo dutiable?
   ए कुवेस्ता बोतिल्या दी प्रोफुमो दयुतीएबल?

7. Can I import this bottle of wine?
   Posso improtare questa bottiglia di vino?
   Posso importarē quēsta bottiglia di vino?
   पोसो इमपोरतारे कुएस्ता बोतिल्या दी वीनो?

8. Yes, this is my health certificate.
   Si, questo è mio certificato di salute.
   Si, Quēsto ē mio cērtificato di salutē,
   सी कुवेस्तो ए मियो चरतीफिकातो दी सालुते।

9. These are my personal belongings?
   Questi sono le mie personale cose?
   Quēsti sono lē miē cosē personalē?
   कुएस्ती सोनो ले मिये कोजे परसोनाले?

10. Do I have to open the bag?
    Devo aprire la borsa?
    Dēvo aprirē la borsa?
    देवो अपरीरे ला बोरसा?

11. Where is the toilet?
    dove è la toletta?
    doovē ē la tolētta?
    दोवे ए ला तोलेत्ता?

12. Is there a coffee shop here?
    E ci una caffeteria qua?
    Ē ci una caffētēria qua?
    ए ची उना काफ़ीतेरिया क्वा?

13. How can I reach hotel Radission?
    Come posso arrivare albergo redission?
    Comē posso arrivarē albērgo radission?
    कोमे पोसो अरीवारे अलबेरगो रेडिसन?

14. How far it is?
    Come lon tano è?
    Comē lon tano ē?
    कोमे लोन तानो ए?

15. Where can I get a taxi?
    dove posso prendere un taxi?
    dovē posso prēndērē un taaxi?
    दोवे पोसो प्रेनदेरे उन तासी?

16. Can I get Indian currency here?
    Posso prendere moneta indiana qua?
    Posso prēndērē monētta indianā quā?
    पोसो प्रेनदेरे मोनेत्ता इनदयाना कव्आ?

17. Do you have traveller's cheques?
    Tu hai assegno turistioo?
    Tu ai assēno turistico?
    तु आइ असेनो तुरीस्तिको?

18. Kindly give me the receipt.
    Mi dai la ricevuta?
    Me dai la ricēvuta?
    मी दाई ला रिचेवुता?

19. How about these US made medicines?
    Come da questi us fa medicine?
    Comē da quēsti us fa medicinē?
    कोमे दा कुएस्ती युस फा मेदिचिने?

20. They are for my personal use.
    Quelli sono per mio personale uso.
    Quēlli sonō pēr mio pērsonalē uso.
    कुएली सोनो प्रेर मियो उसो परसोनाले।

21. Thank god, that I can carry them.
    Grazie dio, che posso portarli.
    Gratsiē dio, chē possō portarli.
    ग्रातसिये दियो के पोसो पोरतारली।

22. Well, kindly guide me to the exit.
    Bene, mi guida alla uscità.
    Bēnē, mi guida alla useitā.
    बेने मि गवीदा अला उसीता।

23. Do you speak English?
    parli inglese?
    parli inglēsē?
    पारली इंगलेजे?

24. Kindly explain my problem to the taxi driver.
    spiega il mio problema al guidatore di taxi.
    Spiēga il mio problēma al guidatorè di taaxi.
    स्पीयेगा इल मियो प्रोबलेमा अल गवीदातोरे दी तासी।

25. Is there a bus or train service to the city?
    cè ci un autous o treno servizia alla città?
    cē ci un cutobus o trēno sērvitsia alla cittā?
    चे सी उन ओतो बुस ओ त्रेनो सरवितसिया अला चित्ता?

Conversation with the taxi driver

1. Can you take me to hotel Radisson.
   Puoi portarmi a albergo radisson.
   pooy portarmi a albērgo radission.
   पोये पोरतारमी आ अलबेरगो रेडिसन।

2. Yes, I have got a booking there.
   Si, ci Ho prenotatao.
   See ci oo prēnotato.
   सी ची ओ प्रेनोतातो

3. How much will you charge?
   Quanto mi farai pagare?
   Quanto mi farāi pagarē?
   कुआन्तो मि फराई पागारे?

4. Three hundred rupees are too much.
   Tre cento rupees sono costa troppo.
   Trē cĕnto rupees sono costa troppo.
   त्रे चेन्तो रूपये सोनो कोस्ता त्रोपो।

5. I have seen the rate list.
   Ho visto il listino prezzi.
   Oo visto il listīnō prētsi.
   ओ विसतो इल लिसतिनो प्रेतसी।

6. Two hundred rupees are enough.
   due cento rupees sono basta.
   dooy cēnto rupees sono baasta.
   दुये चेन्तो रूपये सोनो बासता।

7. O.K., you load this luggage.
   Allova, carici questi bagagli.
   Allora kariki quēsti baagali.
   अलोरा कारीकी कुएस्ती बागाली।

8. How long will it take to reach?
   Da quando è impiegerà arrivare?
   Da quando ē impiē gēraa arrivarē?
   दा कुआन्दो अ इमपेगेरा अरीवारे?

9. Since when you are driving in this city?
   Da quando tu guida in questa citta?
   Da quando tu guidi in quēsta cittā?
   दा कुआन्दो तु गवीदी इन कुएस्ता चित्ता?

10. Can I hire your taxi for a full day?
    Posso noliggiare tuo taxi per un tutto giorno?
    Posso nolēgaarē tuo taxi pēr un tutto giorno?
    पोसो नोलेजारे तुओ तासी पेर उन तुत्तो जोरनो?

11. Will you charge on hourly basis?
    Farei pagare su all'ora base?
    Farēi pagarē soocil'ora bazē?
    फारेई पागारे सु अलोरा बाजे?

12. Or according to distance?
    O secondo a distanza?
    ō sēcondo a distanza?
    ओ सेकोनदो आदीस्तांजा?

13. How can I contact you?
    Come posso contarti?
    Comē posso contatarti?
    कोमे पोसो कोनतातारती?

14. Well, we are almost there.
    Bene, siamo quasi ci.
    Bēnē siamo qasi ci.
    बेने सियामो कुआजी ची ।
15. Thank you for this interesting ride.
    Gratzie per questo interessante passeggiata.
    Gratzie pēr quēsto intērēssantē passēggiata.
    ग्रात्सीए पेर कुएस्तो इत्रजानते पासेजाता ।

At the hotel

1. I hope I have got a reservation.
   Io spero di avere prenotazione.
   Spēro di avērē prēnotazionē.
   सपेरो दी आवेरे प्रेनोतातसीयोने।

2. Yes, I asked for a single bed room
   Si, ho chiesto per letto a una piazza camera.
   Si, ho chiēsto pēr lētto a una piazzā camēra.
   सि ओ किस्तो पेर लेत्तो आ उना पियात्जा कामेरा।

3. I had wired from Singapore.
   avevo collegata da singapore.
   avēvo collēgata da singapore.
   आवेवो कोलेगाता दा सिंगापुर।

4. I sent it about a week ago.
   lo'ho mandato da una settimana fa.
   lo-oo mandatō da una sēttimana fa.
   ला ओ मानदातो दा उना सेतीमाना फा।

5. Oh, thank god that I have got my room.
   oh, graztie dio che ho preso mia camera.
   oh, graztié dio chē oo prēso miā camēra.
   ओ ग्रातसिये दियो के ओ प्रेजो मिया कामेरा।

6. No, I failed to write you in advance.
   No, sono bocciato di collegiarti in anticipo.
   No sono bocciatō di collegiarti in anticipo.
   नो सोनो बुच्चातो दी कोलयारती इन आनतीचिपो।

7. Kindly, try your best.

Provi suo meglio.
Provi suō mēgliō.
प्रोवी सुओ मेलियो।

8. O.K., a double bed room will do.
Bene, una camera matrimoniale servirà.
Bēnē una camēra matri monialē sēriraa.
बेने उना कामेरा मातेरी मोनियाले सेरविरा।

9. How much will it be?
quanto sarà?
quantō saraah?
कुआन्तो सरा?

10. Quite reasonable.
assai vagionevole.
assāi ragionēvolē.
आसाई राजोनेवोले।

11. Oh, it's quite expensive.
oh, È assai costoso.
oh, Ē assāi costōsā.
ओ! ए असाई कोस्तोजो।

12. Does it include any meals?
Include dei pasti?
Include dēi pasti?
इनकलुदे देइ पास्ती?

13. I have to stay for three days.
Devo stare per tre giorni.
Dēvo starē pēr trē giorni.
देवो स्तारे पेर त्रे जोरनी।

14. No, for one night only.

No, per uno notte solo.
No, pēr uno nottē solo.
नो पेर उनो नोते सोलो।

15. It is quite small.
È assai piccolo.
Ē assāi pikoolo.
ए असाई पिक्कोलो।

16. It is not cool.
Non è freddo.
Non ē frēddo.
नान ए फ्रेदो।

17. The window does not face the sea.
la finestra non affronta il mare.
La finēstrā non affronta il marē.
ला फिनेस्त्रा नान अफ्रोन्ता इल मारे?

18. It doesn't appear adequately clean.
Non appare adequatamente chiaro.
non apparē adēquatamēntē kiaro.
नान आपरे आदिकुआतामेन्ते क्यारो।

19. Kindly clean it first.
pulisca questo prima.
pulishka quēsto prima.
पुलीसका कुएस्तो प्रिमा।

20. How can I get some fresh air?
Come posso prendere l'aria fresco?
Comē posso prēndērē l'aria frēsco?
कोमे पोसो प्रेनदेरे लाआरिया फ्रेस्को?

21. Do you have air conditioned rooms?

Tu hai aria condizione camere?
Tu ai ariā conditsionē camēri?
तु आइ आरिया कनदितसियोने कामेरे?

22. What will be the extra charge?
Cosa sarà extra prezzo?
Cosa saraah extra pretsso?
कोजा सारा एस्त्रा प्रेतजो?

23. Can I check out at 10.00 AM?
Posso saldare il conto alle 10 am?
Posso saldarē il conto allē 10 am?
पोसो सालदारे इल कोनतो अले 10 ए एम?

24. Is credit card facility available?
E carta di credito facillita disponibili?
Ē conta di crēdito facilita disponibilē?
ए कारता दी क्रेदितो फाचिलीता दिसपोनीबिले?

25. Does the bank have ATM facility?
Banca ha facillita di ATM banca ha facillita di cassa automatica prelicvi?
Bankā a facillita di cassa automatica prēliēvi?
बानका आ फाचीलिता दी कासा आतोमातीका प्रेलीएवी?

26. Where is my key?
dove le mie chiavi?
dove lē miē kiavi?
दोवे ले मिये क्यावी?

27. Here is my key.
Ecao! e mio chiave?
Ēcco e mio kiavē?
एको ए मियो क्यावे?

28. No, I am a vegetarian.
   no sono vegetariano.
   No sono vēgētariano.
   नो सोनो वेजेत्रयानो।

29. I eat eggs.
   Mangio uovi.
   Mangio uoovi.
   मानजो उवी।

30. Can I order wine in my room?
   Posso ordire vino in mia camera?
   Posso ordirē vino in mia camēra?
   पोसो ओरदीरे वीनो इन मिया कामेरा?

31. Am I allowed to take my lady friends to my room?
   È permisso portare mie amiche a mia camera?
   Ē Pērmēsso portarē mie amica a mia camēra?
   ए प्रेरमेस्सो पोरतारे मिया आमीका आ मिया कामेरा?

32. What are the means of entertainment available here?
   Quali sono i mezzi di divertimento disponsibili qua?
   Quali sono i mētzi di divērtimēnto disponsibile qua?
   क्वाली सोनो इ मेतसी दी दीवेरतीमेन्तो दिसपोनसीबिले क्वा?

33. Hello reception, kindly connect me to phone number........!
   Pronto! ricevimento, Mi connetta a tilefono mumero ....

Pronto! ricēvimēnto mi connētta a telēfono numēro.

प्रोन्तो रीचेवीमेन्तो मि कोनेता आ तेलेफोनो नुमेरो।

34. Send him/her up to my room.
   mandalo/la su a mia camera.
   Manda lo/la su a mia camēra.
   मानदा लो / ला सु आ मिया कामेरा।

35. Tell him/her to wait in the lobby.
   dice lo/la aspettare nel atrio.
   Dicē lo/la aspēttarē nēliatrio.
   दीचे लो / ला आसपेतारे नेल आतोरीयो।

36. I'll be there within half an hour.
   Sarò li all'interno mezza unora.
   Sarooh li all'intērno Metsa un ora.
   सारा ली अल इनतेरनो मेतसा उन ओरा।

37. I will return in the evening.
   Ritornerò nella sera.
   Ritornērooh nēlla sēra.
   रितोरनेरा नेला सेरा।

38. Tell the visitor to come on Monday.
   dice il visitatore di venire a lunedi.
   Dicē il visitatorē di venirē a lunēdi.
   दीचे इल विजितातोरे दी वेनिरे आ लुनेदी।

39. It is room number three or four?
   È camera numero tre o quatrro.
   Ē camēra numēro trē o quatrro.
   ए कामेरा नुमेरो त्रे ओ कुआत्रो।

40. Send me some warm water.

103

Mandami dell'acqua caldo.
Mandami dēll acquā caldo.
मानदामी देला आक्वा कालदो।

41. By what time the lunch will be ready?
Alle che ora il pranzo sara' pronta?
Allē chē ora il pranzo saraah prontā?
अले के ओरा इल प्रानजो सरा प्रोनतो?

42. Uptil what time you are open for the dinner?
Fino che ora apri per la cina?
Fino chē ora apri pēr la cēna?
फिनो के ओरो आपरी पेर ला चेना?

43. What is the dish of the day?
Cosa è il piatto del giorno?
cosā ē il piatto dēl giorno?
कोजा ए इल पियातो देल जोरनो?

44. Kindly serve the meal in my room!
Per favore serva il pasto in mia camera?
Pēr favorē sērva il pasto in mia camēra?
पेर फावोरे सेरवा इल पास्तो इन मिया कामेरा?

45. I am checking out.
Scaldo il conto.
Skaldo il conto.
स्कालदो इल कोनतो।

46. Call a taxi for me.
Chiami un taxi per mi.
Kiami un taxi pēr mē.
कियामी उन तासी पेर मे।

47. Yes, straight to the Airport.
    Si, dritto al'aeroporto.
    Si dritto al'Aēvoporto.
    सी दीरीत्तो अल एरोपोरतो।

At a tourist place

1. Is there any office of tourism department here?
    c'è qualche officio di tourismo depar taminto qua?
    c'èqualkē officio di tourismo dēpartamēnto qua?
    चे कुवालके आफीचियो दी तुरीस्मो दीपारतोमेन्तो क्वा?

2. Yes, I want a tourist guide.
    Si, io voglio guida di turisti.
    Si, io voglio guida di touristi.
    सी इओ वोलीयो गवीदा दी तुरीस्तो।

3. Are you a registered guide?
    Tu sei unq guida assicurato?
    Tu sēi un guida assikurata?
    तु सेई उन गवीदा आसीकुराता?

4. Kindly sow me your I-card.
    per favoure mi mostri tua carta d'identità.
    pēr favarē mi mostri tua karta d'idēntità.
    पेर फावारे मि मोसत्री तुआ कारता दी इनदेन्तिता।

5. How much time will it take to see this place completely?
    Quanto tempo impiegerà a vedere questa luogo completamente?
    Quanto Tēmpo impiēgērah vēdērē quēsta luogo completamēntē.
    कुआन्तो तेम्पो इमपेगेरा आ वेदेरे कुएस्ता लुओगो कोम्प्लेतामेन्तो।

6. I do not have seven days..........will three days do?

   non, ho sette giorni .... tre giorni bastarebbe.

   Non, ho sētte giorni trē.............. giorni basta rēbbē.

   नोन ओ सेते जोरनी त्रे जोरनी बासता रेबे ।

7. Do you charge your fee on daily basis?

   Fai pagare tuo pagamento quotidiano base?

   Fai pagarē tuo pagamēnto quotidiano basē?

   फाई पागारे तुओ पागामेन्तो कोतीदियानो बाजे?

8. How much do you charge for your package of three days?

   quanto fai pagare per tuo pacco di tre giorni?

   Quanto fai pagarē pēr tuo pako di trē giorṇi?

   कुआन्तो फाई पागारे पेर तुओ पांको दी त्रे जोरनी?

9. Ok, get tickets for the three of us.

   Bene, prandi biglietto per tre di noi.

   Bēnē prēndi biliētto pēr trē di no-e.

   बेने प्रेनदी बिलियेतो पेर त्रे दी नोई ।

10. Do you know the history of this monument with details?

    Tu sai la storia di questo monumento con dettaglio.

    Tu sai la storia di quēsto monumēnto con dettalio.

    तु साई ला स्तोरिया दी कुएस्तो मोनुमेन्तो कोन देतालियो ।

11. How old it is?
    Quanti anni ha?
    Quanti anni ha?
    कुआन्ती आनी आ?
12. Was the king assassinated?
    Fu assassinato il rè?
    Foo assassinto il rē?
    फु आसासिनातो इल रे?
13. Did the queen die a natural death?
    La regiṇa era morta naturale morte?
    la rējina ēra morta naturalē mortē?
    ला रेजिना एरा मोरता नातुराले मोरते?
14. Did the prince rule after the king's death?
    il principe governa dopo il rè era morto?
    il principe govērna dopo il rē ēra morto?
    इल प्रिनचिपे गोवेरना दोपो इल रे एरा मोरतो?
15. How many wives did he have?
    Quante mogli lui ha avuto?
    Quantē moli lui ha avuto?
    कुआन्ते मोली लुई आ आवुतो?
16. Tell me the exact period of his rule.
    dimmi il periodo esatto di suo governo.
    dimmi il ēsatto pēriodo di suo govērno.
    दीमी इल एजातो पेरीओदो दीसुओ गोवेरनो।
17. Did he have any brother?
    Ha avuto fratili?
    ha avuto fratēlli?
    आ आवुतो फ़ातेली?

18. Was he enthroned during his father's life time itself?
    Era durante suo padre vita tempo?
    Ēra durantē suo padrē vita tēmpo?
    एरा दुरान्ते सुओ पादरे विता तेम्पो?

19. Who was the actual heir?
    chi era il vero erede?
    ki ēra il vēro ērēdē?
    की एरा इल वेरो ऐरेदे?

20. Why does this arch stand separately?
    perchè questo arco sostegno separatamente?
    Pērchē quēsto arco sostēno sēparatamēntē?
    पेरके कुएस्तो आरको सोसतेनो सेपारातामेन्ते?

21. Let's now enter the main structure.
    Entriamo adesso il principle struttura.
    Ēntriano adēsso il principlē struttura.
    एन्त्रामो अदेसो इल प्रिनचिपले स्त्रुतुरा।

22. Let's choose the right path.
    Scegliamo il vero strada.
    Sayliamo il vēro strada.
    सेलयामो इल वेरो स्त्रादा।

23. Do we have to ascend any staircases?
    Dobbiamo salire scala?
    Dobbiamo salirē skala?
    दोब्बयामो सालीरे स्काला?

24. Roughly how many steps?
    Roughly how many steps?
    Roodēmēntē quantē scalē?

रोदेमेन्ते कुआन्ते स्काले?
25. Is it a one way route?
È unico percorso?
Ē uniko pērcorso?
ए उनीको पेरकोरसो?
26. Is the exit route rather tough?
l'uscita percorso piuttosto duro?
l'uscita pērcorso piuttosto dooro?
ल उसीता पेरकोरसो पिओतोस्तो दोरो?
27. Where does it open?
dove loapra?ˑ
Dovē lo aprā?
दोवे लो आपरा?
28. Were any foreign engineers involved in this construction?
Furono dei ingegneri stanieri involuto in questo costruzione?
Fu roono dēi ingēnēri straniēri involuto in quēsto costruzionē?
फुरोनो देई इनजेनेरी स्त्रानियेरी इनवोलुतो इल कुएस्तो कोसत्रुजियोने?
29. Can you read the inscription on this tomb?
Puoai liggere il iscrizione su questa tomba?
po-oy lēggērē il iscritsonē su quēsta tomba?
पोये लेजेरे इल इसक्रिजियोने सु कुएस्ता तोम्बा?
30. Tell me what it says?
Dimmi cosa dice?
Di-mmi cosa dicē?

110

दी मी कोजा दीचे?

31. Does this minaret signify some thing special?
Questo minarete significa qualcosa semplice?
Quēsto minarētē sinifica qualkosa sēmplicē?
कुएस्तो मीनारेते सिनीफिका कुआलकोजा सेम्प्लीचे?

32. Is it necessary to ignite incense stick here?
È necessario accendere incenso gambo qua?
Ē nēcēssario accēndērē incēnso gambo qua?
ए नेचेसारियो आचेन्देरे इनसेन्सो गाम्बो कुवा?

33. Where does this tunnel lead to?
Dove questa galleria pasizione a?
Dovē quēsta gallēria positsione ā?
दोवे कुएस्ता गालेरिया पोजितसिओने आ?

34. Was it constructed later on?
Costruì più avanti?
Costruii piu avānti?
कोस्त्रुई पियु आवान्ती?

35. Was the king liked by the people?
Fu il re è piaciuto dai popoli?
Fu il rē ē piaciuto daai popoli?
फु इल रे ए पियाचुतो दाई पोपोली?

36. Can I see through that ventilator?
Posso vedere traverso questo ventilatore?
Po-sso vēdērē travērso quēsto vēntilaatorē?
पोसो वेदेरे त्रावेरसो कुएस्तो वेनतिलातोरे?

37. What do you call this structure in Hindi?
Come si dice questa struttura in Hindi?
Comē si dicē quēsta struttura in Hindi?

111

कोमे सी दीचे कुएस्ता स्त्रुततुरा इन हिन्दी?

38. And what is the name of this material?
E come si chima questo materiale?
Ē comē si kyaamo quēsto matērialē?
ए कोमे सी कियामो कुएस्तो मातेरियाले?

39. Can one reach outside the dome?
si può arrivare fuori la copola?
Si pu-oo arrivarē fuori la cupola?
सी पो अरीवारे फोरी ला कुपोला?

40. Are these walls hollow?
questi muri sono cavi?
quēsti muri sono kavi?
कुएस्ती मुरी सोनो कावी?

41. Are these real solid?
Questi vero solido?
quēsti vēro solido?
कुएस्ती वेरो सोलीदो?

42. Were these made deliberately so?
Furono fatto deliberatamente?
Fu-rono fatto delibēratamēntē?
फु रोनो फात्तो देलीब्रातामेन्तो?

43. How much time it took to complete?
Quanto tempo impiega di completare?
quanto tēmpo impiēga di complētarē?
कुआन्तो तेम्पो इमपियेगा दी कोम्प्लेतारे?

44. Were local artists and labourers employed?
Furono local artisti e lavorator impiegato?
Furono lokali artisti ē lavoratori impiēgato?

112

फुरोनो लोकाली आरतीसती ए लावोरातोरी इमपेगातो?

45. Who was the chief architect?
    chi era il capo architetto?
    ki ēra il kapo arkitetto?
    की एरा इल कापो आरकीतेत्तो?

46. Whose statue is this?
    di chi statua e questa?
    di ki statua ē quēsta?
    दी की स्तात्तुआ ए कुएस्ता?

47. Can I go into sanctum sanctorum of the temple?
    posso andare nell del tempolo?
    po-sso andarē nell dēl tēmpolo?
    पोसो आन्दारे नेल देल तेम्पोलो?

48. What material this is made of?
    Cosa materiale questo è fatto di?
    ko-sa matēriale quēsto ē fatto di?
    को जा मातेरीयाले कुएस्तो ए फात्तो दी?

49. Which God does this temple belong to?
    Quale dio questo tempolo appar tene a?
    Qualē dio quēsto tēmpolo appartēnē a?
    कुवाले दियो कुएस्तो तेम्पोलो अपारतेने आ?

50. Do we have to take our shoes off?
    Dobbiamo togliersi nostre scarpe?
    Do-biamo toliērsi nostrē scarpē?
    दो बियाम़ो तोलीएरसी नोसत्रे स्कारपे?

51. Is there some eating place here?
    Ci qualchi luogo di mangiare qua?
    Ci qualkay luogo di mangiarē qua?

ची कुआलके लुओगो दी मानजारे कुवा?

52. Is the prasad given to everyone?
da il prasad a ogni persona?
Da il prasad a ooni pērsonē?
दा इल प्रसाद अ ओनी पेरसोने?

53. Is it palatable for a foreigner?
È gustoso per un straniero?
Ē goostoso pēr un straniēro?
ए गुस्तोजो पेर उन स्त्रानीएरो?

54. And adequate in quantity too?
E adeguato in quantita anche?
Ē adēguato in quantita ankay?
ए आदेगुवातो इन कुआनतिता आनके?

55. How far is the beach?
Quanto è lontano la spiaggia?
Quanto ē lontano la spiaja?
कुआनतो ए लोनतानो ला स्पयाजा?

56. Does the management accept any monetary contributions?
La amministraziane accetta monetario contributo?
la amministratsionē accētta monētario contribu-to?
ला आमीनिस्त्रातसियोने आचेता मोनेतारियो कोनत्रीबुतो?

57. Then, where is this counter?
Allora, dove e questo banco?
Allora, dovē ē quēsto banco?
आलोरा दोवे ए कुएस्तो बानको?

58. Can we hire swimming costume here?

114

Possiamo noleggiare costume da bagno qua?
Possiamo nolē ggiarē costomē da bano qua?
पोसयामो नोले जारे कोसतुमे दा बानो कुवा?

59. Is there facility for sun bathing?
C'è facalita per bagno di sole?
C'è facilita pēr bano di solē?
चे फाचीलिता पेर बानो दी सोले?

60. Are only foreigners allowed?
Solo stranieri sono permessi?
Solo straniēri sono permēssi?
सोलो स्त्रानीएरी सोनो पेरमेसी?

61. How does one reach that island?
Come si arriva quella isola?
comē si arriva quēlla isola?
कोमे सी अरीवा कुवेला इजोला?

62. By steamer, motor boat or ferry?
Da piroscafo, motoscalo, otraghetteo?
Da piroskafo, motoskalo, otraghetto?
दा पिरोस्काफो, मोतोस्कालो, ओत्रगेत्तो?

63. Do you have any of your friends in Manali?
Tu hai tuoi amici in Manali?
Tu ai tu-o-i amici in Manali?
तु आइ तुओई आमीची इन मानाली?

64. Yes, we want to visit that hilly area also.
Si, vogliamo visitare collinoso area anche.
Si, voliamo visitarē collinoso area ankē.
सी वालयामो विजितारे कोलीनोजो आरिया आनके।

65. Thank you very much for your excellent job.

Graztie mille per tuo eccellente lavoro.
Gratsie millē pēr tuo eccēllēntē lavoro.
ग्रातसिये मिल्ले पेर तुओ एचीलेन्ते लावोरो।

66. Here is your fee.......keep the change.
Ecco e tuo pagaminto .... tengi il resto.
Ēko ē tuo pagamēnto .... ten-gi il rēsto.
एको ए तुओ पागामेन्तो तेंगी इल रेस्तो।

General sentences for every day use

1. Hello, how are you?
   Ciao, come stai?
   Ca-ao komē sta-e?
   चा ओ कोमे स्ताई?

2. I am fine.
   sto bene.
   sto bēnē.
   स्तो बेने।

3. Bring me coffee.
   Portami un caffe.
   Portami un caffē.
   पोरतामी उन काफे।

4. Stay there.
   Stai lì.
   Stai lì.
   स्ताई ली।

5. Come here.
   Vieni qua.
   viēni qua.
   वीयेनी कुवा।

6. Go inside.
   Vai interno.
   Vai intērno.

वाई इनतेरना।

7. Wait in the lawn.
   Aspetti nel tappeto erboso.
   Aspētti nēl tappēto ērboso.
   असपेत्ती नेल तापेतो एरबोजो।

8. Meet at the gate.
   incontri al canallo.
   incontri al canallo.
   इनकोनत्री अल कनालो।

9. Walk on the pavement.
   Cammini sul paviminto.
   kammini sul pavimēnto.
   कामीनी सुल पावीमेन्तो।

10. It is not a parking place.
    non è parcheggio.
    Non ē parkēgio.
    नोन ए पारकेजीयो।

11. The pen is in the box.
    la penna è nella scatola.
    la pēnna ē nēlla skatola.
    ला पेन्ना ए नेल्ला स्कातोला।

12. Your shoe is under the table.
    Tue scarpe è sotto la tavola.
    Tuē scarpē ē sotto la tavola.
    तुए स्कारपे ए सोतो ला तावोला।

13. The green stripe is below the white one.
    la verdi striscia è sotto bianco striscia.
    la vērdi striscia ē sotto bianko striscia.

ला वेरदी स्त्रासिया ए सोतो बियानको स्त्रासियां ।

14. Lift the ball from the ground.
    Sollevi la palla dalla terra.
    Sollēvi la palla dalla tērra.
    सोलेवी ला पाल्ला दाला तेररा ।

15. Take it.
    prender lo.
    prēndērlo.
    प्रेनदेरलो ।

16. Give me the paper.
    dammi il foglio.
    dammi il foglio.
    दामी इल फोलिया ।

17. It is cold outside.
    È freddo fuori.
    Ē frēddo foo-ori.
    ए फ्रेदो फोरी ।

18. It is rather humid inside.
    È piuttosto umido interno.
    Ē piuttosto umido intērno.
    ए पियोतोसंतो उमीदो इनतेरनो ।

19. It still appears dirty.
    È ancora appare sporco.
    Ē ankora apparē sporko.
    ए अनकोरा आपारे स्पोरको ।

20. She has not come yet.
    lei Non viene ancora.
    lei Non viēnē ankora.

119

लेई नान वियेने अनकोरा।

21. Yes, now it appears clean.
    Si addeso lo appare chiaro.
    Si addēeso lo apparē kiaro.
    सी आदेसो लो आपारे कियारो।

22. Go upstairs.
    Vai al piano superiore.
    Vai al piano supēriorē.
    वाई अल पियानो सोपेरीओरे।

23. Come downstairs
    Vieni al piano inferiore.
    Viēni al piano infēriorē.
    वियेनी अल पियानो इनफेरीओरे।

24. I want a washer man.
    Voglio un lavandaio.
    Voglio un lavanda-io.
    वोलियो उन लावानदा ओ।

25. Is there a laundry nearby?
    C'è una lavanderia vicino?
    c'è una lavandēria vicino?
    चे उना लावेनदेरीयो विचिनो?

26. Can she iron this shirt well?
    lei può stirare guista camizia bene?
    lēi poo-u stirarē quēsta kamicia bēnē?
    लेई पो स्तीरारे कुएस्ता कामीचिया बेने?

27. Call her quickly.
    Chiama la rapidaminte.
    ki-ama la rapidamēntē.

क्यामा ला रापीदामेन्ते ।

28. It is getting late.
    È ritardi.
    Ē ritardi.
    ए रीतारदी ।

29. It is quite early.
    È più presto.
    Ē pi-oo prēsto.
    ए पियो प्रेस्तो ।

30. Run faster
    Corri veloce.
    Corri vēlocē.
    कोरी वेलोचे ।

31. Walk slowly.
    cammini piano.
    kammini piano.
    कामीनी पियानो ।

32. The newspaper is on the bed.
    il giornali è sul litto.
    il giornali ē sul lētto.
    इल जोरनाली ए सुल लेत्तो ।

33. The dictionary is above the magazine.
    il dizionario è sopra la rivista.
    il ditsionario ē sopra la rivista.
    इल दितस्योनारीयो ए सोपरा ला रीविस्ता ।

34. The post office is in front.
    il officio postale è in davanti.
    il officio postalē ē in davanti.

इल आफीचो पोसताले ए इन दावान्ती।

35. What lies behind it?
    Cosa ce dietro.
    koza c'ē diētro.
    कोजा चे दीएत्रो।

36. There is a banyan tree beside the mosque.
    c'è un albero di banyan dietro moschea.
    c'è un albēro di banyan diētro moska.
    चे उन अलबेरो दी बनियान दीएत्रो मोसका।

37. Are you from Oriental Travels?
    sei da oriental travels?
    Sēi da oriēntal travels?
    सेई दा ओरीएन्ताल ट्रेवल्स?

38. Will this telephonic talk do?
    Serve questa conversaztione telephoinco?
    Sērvē quēsta convēr satsionē tēlēphoniko?
    सेरवे कुएस्ता कोनवेरजातसियोने तेलीफोनीको?

39. We want to visit Nainital.
    Vogliamo visitare Nainital.
    Voliamo visitarē Nainital.
    वोलीयामो विजितारे नेनीताल।

40. For four adults.
    per quattro adulti.
    pēr quattro adulti.
    पेर कुआत्रो अदुलती।

41. No, there are no children.
    No, ci sono no bambini.
    No, ci sono no bambini.

नो ची सोनो नो बामबीनी।

42. Yes, no one is under twenty five.
Si, nessuno è sotto 25 anni.
Si, nēssuno ē sotto 25 anni.
सी नेसुनो ए सोतो 25 आनी।

43. For four days including up and own journey?
per quattro giorni compresso su e giù viaggio?
Pēr quattro giorni comprēsso su ē giu viaggio?
पेर कुआत्रो जोरनी कोमप्रेस्सो सु ए जु वियाजो?

44. Including all the meals?
Compreso tutta la pasta?
Comprēso tutta la pasta?
कोमप्रेस्सो तुत्ता ला पासता?

45. Excluding lunches?
Excludo pranzo?
Excludo prantso?
एस्क्लुदो प्रानजो?

46. You are asking for too much.
tu stai chiedendo per molto.
tu sta-ai kiēdēndo pēr motto.
तु स्ताई केदेनदो पेर मोलतो।

47. No, it's not reasonable.
No, non è ragionevole.
No, non ē ragionēvolē.
नो, नोन ए राजोनेवोले।

48. Which vehicle will you provide?
Quali veicolo provvederai?
qualē vēicolo provvēdēraai.

कुआले वेईकोलो प्रोवेद्राई।

49. Yes, an A.C. Qualis will be better.
Si, un A.C. qualis sarà meglio.
Si un A.C. qualis saraah mēleo.
सी उन ए सी कुआलीस सरा मेलयो।

50. It is a public telephone booth?
È una cabina telephonica publica?
Ē una cabina tēlēphonica publica?
ए उना काबीना तेलीफोनिका पुबलीका?

51. Can I make an ISD call from here?
Posso fare ISD chiama da qua?
Posso farē ISD kiamo da qua?
पोसो फारे आई एस डी कियामो दा कुआ?

52. And local calls well?
E anche telefonata urbana?
Ē anke tēlefonata urbana?
ए आनके तेलीफोनाता उरबाना?

53. Do you have internet facility also?
Avete facilita di internet anche?
Avētē facilita di intērnēt anchē?
आवेते फाचिलीता दी इनतरनेत आनके?

54. Can I check my E-mail here?
Posso vedere mia posta elettronica qua?
Possō vēdērē mia posta ēlēttronica qua?
पोसो वेदेरे मिया पोसता इलेत्रोनिका कुवा?

55. At what rate you charge for net surfing?
Quanto prezzo prendi per netto surfing?
Quanto prēzzo prēndi pēr nētto surfing?

कुआन्तो प्रेत्जो प्रेंरदी पेर नेत्तो सरफिंग?

56. So you sell antiques….?
    Allora, vendi antichitè?
    Allora, vendi antikitē?
    आलोरा वेन्दी आनतीके?

57. And modern art works?
    E moderno arte lavoro?
    Ē modērno artē lavoro?
    ए मोदेरनो आरते लावोरो?

58. How much is that silken cap?
    quanti è questo silicio capello?
    Quanti ē quēsto silici-o capēllo?
    कुआन्ती ए कुएस्तो सिलीचो कापेलो?

59. No, the red one behind the orange one.
    No il rosso è dietro il aran-cione.
    No il rosso ē diētro il arancionē.
    लो इल रोजो ए दीएत्रो इल अरनचोने

60. My god, is it so expensive?
    Mio dio È molto costoso?
    me-o de-o Ē molto costoso?
    मियो दियो ए मोलतो कोसतोजो?

61. Some thing cheaper?
    Qualcosa meno caro?
    qualcosa mēno caro?
    कुआलकोजा मेनो कारो?

62. Does this bronze piece qualify as an antique?
    il Bronzo pezzo si qualifica come un anti chità?
    il bronzo pētso si qualifika comē un antikità?

इल ब्रोनजो पेत्सो सी कुआलीफिका कामे उन आनतिकीता?

63. O. K., pack it.
Bene stipi lo.
Bēnē stipilo.
बेने स्तीपीलो ।

64. Don't delay.
Non ritardi.
Non ritardi.
नोन रीतारदी ।

65. Tell him to keep his fingers off the piece.
lo dici mettere suo dito lontano da pezzo.
Lo dici mēttērē suo dito lontano da pētso.
लो दीची मेतेरे सुओ दीतो लोनतानो दा पे़तसो ।

66. My shoes need polish.
Mie scarpe bisognio lucido.
miē skarpē bisognio lucido.
मिये स्कारपे बिजोनियो लुचिदो ।

67. I need a hair cut.
Ho bisognio di tagliere i capelli.
oo Bisoznio di tagliere i capēlli.
ओ बिजोनियो दी तालियारे इ कापेल्ली ।

68. Will I have to go to saloon?
doverò andare a saloon?
dovērooh andaare a saloon?
दोवेरो आन्दारे आ सालुन?

69. What do you mean?
Cosa tu vuol dire?

126

coza tu vuol dirē?
कोजा तु वोल दीरे?

70. Why are you worried?
Perchè tu sei preoccupato?
Pērchē tu sēi prēoccupato?
पेरके तु सेई प्रेअकुपाता?

71. How do you cook it?
Come cucini lo?
Comē Cucini lo?
कोमे कुचीनी लो?

72. Where did you get it?
dovē lo hai prēso?
dovē lo hai prēso?
दोवेलो आई प्रेजो?

73. Which of these is yours?
Quali di questo è tuo?
qualē di quēsto ē tuo?
कुआले दी कुएस्तो ए तुओ?

74. When do we go?
Quando andiamo?
quando andiamo?
कुआन्दो अन्दयामो?

75. Sharpen this pencil.
affili questa mattita.
affili quēsta matita.
आफीली कुएस्ता मातीता।

76. What is the matter?
Cosa è il questione?

127

Cosa ē il quēstionē?
कोजा ए इल कुएस्तीओने?

77. It does not sound good.
Non lo fa rumore bene.
Non lo fa romoorē bēnē.
नान लो फा रोमोरे बेने।

78. I am ready for last two hours.
Sono pronto per da due ore.
Sono prontō pēr da duē orē.
सोनो प्रोनतो पेर दा दुए ओरे।

79. I don't believe it.
non lo credo.
Non lo crēdo.
नोन लो क्रेदो।

Italian Vocabulary

1.	Address	Indirizzo	*Indiritso*	इन्दिरित्सो
2.	Agriculture	Agricoltura	*Agrikoltura*	आग्रीकुल्तुरा
3.	Anger	Rabbia	*Rab-bia*	राब्बिया
4.	Animal	Animale	*Animalē*	अनीमाले
5.	Apology	Scuse	*skuzē*	स्कूजे
6.	To accept	accettare	*accēttarē*	आच्चेत्तारे
7.	To act	Recitare	*rēcitarē*	रेचितारे
8.	To add	aggiungere	*ajunjērē*	आजुङ्गनेरे
9.	To admire	ammirare	*ammirarē*	आम्मीरारे

129

10.	To agree	Essere d'accordo	essērē d'akordo	एस्सेरे द्याकोर्दो
11.	Baby	Bambino	bambino	बम्बीनो
12.	Bachelor	Scapolo	skapolo	स्कापोलो
13.	Back	Parte posteriore	partē postēriiorē	पार्ते पोस्तेरीओरे
14.	Backbone	Spina dorsale	spina dorsalē	स्पीना दुर्साल
15.	Backyard	Cortile	cortilē	कोर्तीले
16.	To bow	All'arco	inkinarē/allarko	अलार्को
17.	To bath	bagno	bano/farē un bone	बन्यो
18.	To beat	battere	Battērē	बत्तेरे
19.	To beg	Elemosinare	kiēdērē ēlēmosinare	इलेमोसीनारे
20.	To begin	cominciare	Kominclarē	कमीन्चारे
21.	Cow	Mucca	Mukka	मुक्का
22.	Crime	Crimine	Kriminē	क्रिमीने

		Il raccolto	Il Rakolto	इल राकोलतो
23.	Crop			
24.	Crow	Cornacchia	Kornacia	कुर्नाचा
25.	Crown	Corona	Korona	कोरोना
26.	To clean	pulire	Pulirē	पुलीरे
27.	To close	Scontrarsi	Skontrarsi	स्कोन्त्रारसी
28.	To collect	raccogliere	Rakoliērē	राकोलीआरे
29.	To come	venire	Vēnirē	वेनिरे
30.	To complain	Lamentarsi	Lamēntarsi	लमेन्तारसी
31.	Dog	Cane	Kanē	कानेे
32.	Door	Portello	Portā	पोरतालो
33.	Doubt	Dubbio	Dubbio	डुब्यो
34.	Dozen	Dozzina	dozzina	दोज़िना

131

35.	Dream	Sogno	*sonoo*	सोनो
36.	To desire	Desiderare	*dēsidērarē*	देजीदेरारे
37.	To die	morire	*morirē*	मोरिरे
38.	To dig	Scavare	*skavarē*	स्कावारे
39.	To dip	Tuffarsi	*tuffarsi*	तुफारसी
40.	To disagree	non essere d'accordo	*non ēssērē d'ałordo*	नान एस्सेरे दाकोरदो
41.	Event	Evento	*Ēvēnto*	ईवेन्तो
42.	Eye	Occhio	*okio*	ओक्यो
43.	Eye brow	sopracciglio	*soprācilio*	सोपराचिलियो
44.	Eye lashes	Cigli	*cili*	चिलियो
45.	To eat	mangiare	*Mangiarē*	मानजारे
46.	To educate	Istruire	*istruirē*	स्त्रुइरे

132

47.	To elect	Eleggere	*elēggērē*	एलेजरे
48.	To embarrass	imbarazzare	*imbaratsarē*	इम्बारत्सारे
49.	Face	Faccia	*Faccia*	फाच्चा
50.	Fair	Giusto	*zoosto*	जुस्तो
51.	Farm	Podere	*podērē*	पोदेरे
52.	Father	Padre	*padrē*	पादरे
53.	To fail	bocciare	*bocciarē*	बुचारे
54.	To faint	Svenire	*svenirē*	ज्वनीरे
55.	To fall	cadere	*kadērē*	कादेरे
56.	To fasten	fissarsi	*Fissarsi*	फिस्सार्सी
57.	To fear	timere	*tēmērē*	तेमेरे
58.	Grape	uva	*uva*	उआ

133

59.	Grave	tomba	*tomba*	तोम्बा
60.	Guard	guardia	*guardiā*	गुआरदा
61.	Guest	ospite	*Ospitē*	ओसपीते
62.	Gum	gomma	*gomma*	गोम्मा
63.	To guide	guidare	*guidarē*	गुयीदारे
64.	To guard	proteggere	*proteğğārē*	प्रोतेज़रे
65.	To go	andare	*andarē*	आन्दारे
66.	Home	Casa	*kasa*	काज़ा
67.	Honey	miele	*miēlē*	मिएले
68.	Horn	Corno	*korno*	कोरनो
69.	Horse	Cavallo	*kavallo*	कावाल्लो
70.	Hour	Giro	*viajoc*	ज्याज़ो

134

71.	To hide	nascondersi	naskondersi	नासकोन्देरसी
72.	To hold	tenere	tēnērē	तेनेरे
73.	To honour	onorare	onorarē	ओनोरारे
74.	To hug	abbracciare	abbraciarē	आब्राचारे
75.	Importance	Importanza	Importantsa	इम्पुरतान्जा
76.	Information	informazioni	informatsioni	इन्फोरमातसियोनी
77.	To identify	identificare	identifikarē	इदेन्तीफिकारे
78.	To ignore	ignorare	ignorarē	इग्नोरारे
79.	To imagine	immaginare	immaginarē	इमाजीनारे
80.	Jewellery	gioiēlli	Gioiēlli	जोइएल्ली
81.	Joke	Scherzo	skhertso	स्केरत्सो
82.	Judgement	Giudizio	Giuditsio	जुदितिसियो

135

83.	To joke	scherzare	*skhertsarē*	स्केजारे
84.	To judge	giudicare	*Jiudikarē*	जुदीकारे
85.	To jump	saltare	*Saltarē*	सालतारे
86.	Key	Chiave	*kiave*	क्यावे
87.	Knife	coltello	*koltello*	कोलतेल्लो
88.	Knot	Nodo	*nodo*	नोदो
89.	Knee	Ginocchio	*Ginokio*	जिनोक्यो
90.	To kiss	baciare	*baciarē*	बाच्चारे
91.	To kneel	inginocchiarsi	*inginokiarsi*	इन्जीनोक्याआरसी
92.	To knock	bussare	*bussarē*	बुजारे
93.	To know	sapere	*saperē*	सापेरे
94.	Lady	Signora	*sinora*	सिनोरा

136

95.	Lamb	Agnello	*anēllo*	अन्नलो
96.	Land	Terra	*Tērra*	तेर्रा
97.	To lay	situarsi	*tēndērē*	सितुआरसी
98.	To lead	condurre	*kondurrē*	कोन्दुर्रे
99.	To leak	divulgare	*divulgarē*	दिव्हुलगारे
100.	To leap	saltare	*saltarē*	सालतारे
101.	Magic	magia	*maja*	माजा
102.	Magnet	magnete	*magnētē*	मागनेते
103.	Maid	domestica	*domēstika*	दोमेस्तीका
104.	To meet	incontrare	*inkontrarē.*	इन्कोन्तरारे
105.	To misguide	sviare	*sviarē*	स्वीआरे
106.	To miss	mancare	*mankarē*	मान्कारे

137

107.	To misunderstand	dis capire	*Dis kapirē*	डिस् कापिरे
108.	To mix	mescolare	*Mēskolarē*	मेस्कुलारे
109.	Name	Nome	*Nomē*	नोमे
110.	Nationality	Nazionalità	*natsionalite*	नाज़ोनालिता
111.	Nature	Natura	*Natura*	नातुरा
112.	To nag	nag	*Tormēntarē*	तोर्मेंतरे
113.	To nap	pelo	*Pisolino*	पेलो
114.	To need	bisognare	*Bisognarē*	बिज़ोनारे
115.	To notify	informare	*Informarē*	इनफारमारे
116.	Onion	Cipolla	*cipolla*	चिपोला
117.	Owl	Gufo	*Gufo*	गुफो
118.	To offer	Offrire	*offrirē*	ओफ्रीरे

119.	To ooze	Stillare	*Stillarē*	स्तिलारे
120.	To open	Aprirsi	*aprirē*	आपरिरे
121.	To order	Ordine	*ordirē*	ओर्दिरे
122.	Pain	Dolore	*Dolorē*	दोलोरे
123.	Palm	Palma	*palma*	पालमा
124.	Parrot	Pappagallo	*pappallo*	पापालो
125.	Patient	Paziente	*Paisiēnte*	पाज़ीएन्ते
126.	Peacock	Peacock	*pavonē*	पावोने
127.	To pacify	Pacify	*kalmarē*	कालमारे
128.	To paint	Vernicare	*Vērnikarē*	वेर्नीकारे
129.	To pass	Passare	*Passarē*	पासारे
130.	To pay	Pagare	*pagarē*	पागारे

139

131.	Quality	qualità	*qualitā*	क्वालीता
132.	Queen	Regina	*reglina*	रेजीना
133.	Question	Domanda	*Domānda*	दोमान्दा
134.	To quard	quard	*quard*	क्वार्द
135.	To question	domandare	*domandarē*	दोमान्दारे
136.	To quit	lasciare	*lasciarē*	लासारे
137.	Rabbit	Coniglio	*konilio*	कोनीलियो
138.	Race	Corsa	*korsa*	कोरसा
139.	Reason	ragione	*ragionē*	राजयोने
140.	To rescue	salvare	*Salvarē*	सालवारे
141.	To rest	riposarsi	*riposarsi*	रिपोजारसी
142.	To return	ritornare	*Ritornarē*	रितोरनारे

143.	To ride	guidare	*guidarē*	गुयीदारे
144.	Sacred	Sacro	*sakro*	साक्रो
145.	Salary	Stipendio	*stipēndio*	स्तीपेन्दिओ
146.	Salt	Sale	*salē*	साले
147.	To sing	cantare	*kantarē*	कानतारे
148.	To sink	affondare	*affondarē*	आफ़ुन्दारे
149.	To sit	sedersi	*Sēdērsi*	सेदेरसी
150.	To slap	schiaffeggiare	*skiaffēggiarē*	स्कीयाफेज्जारे
151.	To sleep	dormire	*dormirē*	दोरमीरे
152.	Thing	Cosa	*Coza*	कोसा
153.	Thigh	Coscia	*koscia*	कोसिया
154.	Thousand	Mille	*Millē*	मिल्ले

141

155.	To talk	Parlare	Parlarē	पारलारे
156.	To tap	Sfruttare	sfruttarē	स्फ्रुत्तारे
157.	To tape	Registrare	rēgistrarē	रजिस्त्रारे
158.	To tattoo	Tatuare	tatuarē	ताटुआरे
159.	To teach	Insegnare	insēnarē	इनसेनारे
160.	Ultimatum	Ultimatum	Ultimatum	अल्तिमेतम
161.	Umbrella	Ombrello	ombrēllo	अम्ब्रेलो
162.	To understand	Capire	kapirē	कापिरे
163.	To undress	Spogliarsi	spoliarsi	स्पोल्यारसी
164.	To unite	Unire	Unirē	उनीरे
165.	To unload	Scaricare	skarikarē	स्कारिकारे
166.	Vegetable	Verdura	verdura	वेरदुरा

167.	Vehicle	Veicolo	*veicolo*	वेईकोलो
168.	Village	Villaggio	*villajio*	वीलाजो
169.	Violet	Viola	*viola*	विओला
170.	To vacate	sgomberare	*sgombērarē*	स्गाम्बेरारे
171.	To vary	Variare	*variarē*	वरीआरे
172.	To violate	Violare	*violarē*	विओलारे
173.	To vote	Votare	*votarē*	वातारे
174.	Water	Acqua	*akqua*	अक्वा
175.	Wave	Onda	*on-da*	ओन्दा
176.	Wax	Cera	*cēra*	चेरा
177.	Weapon	Arma	*Arma*	आरमा
178.	To weigh	pesare	*Pēsarē*	पेसारे

143

179.	To whip	sbattere	*Sbatterē*	ज्वातेरे
180.	To whisper	Sussurrare	*sussurrorē*	सुसुरारे
181.	To whistle	Fischiare	*Fiskiare*	फिस्क्यारे